Victoria (1868–1935)   Maud (1869–1938)

Henry, Duke of Gloucester (1900–74)   George, Duke of Kent   John (1905–19)
& Lady Alice Montagu-Douglas-Scott   (1902–42)
(1901–2004)   & Marina of Greece
(1906–68)

Margaret (1930–2002)
& Anthony Armstrong-Jones, 1st Earl of Snowdon (1930–)

Edward, Earl of Wessex   David, Viscount Linley   Lady Sarah Armstrong-Jones
(1964–)   (1961–)   (1964–)
& Sophie Rhys-Jones   & the Hon. Serena Stanhope   & Daniel Chatto
(1965–)   (1970–)   (1979–)

Lady Louise Windsor   James, Viscount Severn
(2003–)   (2007–)

This limited edition has
been personally signed by
ANDREW MORTON

WILLIAM & CATHERINE

WILLIAM & CATHERINE

THEIR LIVES, THEIR WEDDING

ANDREW MORTON

Michael O'Mara Books Limited

First published in Great Britain in 2011 by
Michael O'Mara Books Limited
9 Lion Yard
Tremadoc Road
London SW4 7NQ

A CIP catalogue record for this book is available from the British Library.

Papers used by Michael O'Mara Books Limited are natural, recyclable
products made from wood grown in sustainable forests. The manufacturing
processes conform to the environmental regulations of the country of origin.

ISBN: 978-1-84317-621-3

1 3 5 7 9 10 8 6 4 2

www.mombooks.com

William and Catherine: Their Lives, Their Wedding is also available as
an audiobook, read by Phyllida Nash. Visit http://www.audiogo.co.uk/
royalwedding for more information about the CD and download release.

Text design: Ana Bjezancevic
Picture research: Judith Palmer
Endpaper calligraphy: Patrick Knowles

Printed and bound in Italy by L.E.G.O.

CONTENTS

WILLIAM OF WALES

The Path of the Prince

e was born in the Lindo Wing of St Mary's Hospital in West London on 21 June 1982. In August he was christened William Arthur Philip Louis, although he became known affectionately as 'Wombat' to those close to him. And that, you might have thought, would have been that, if it were not for the fact that he was also known, formally, as 'His Royal Highness Prince William of Wales', and that, being the firstborn son of the Prince of Wales, he had become, by the simple fact of his birth, second in line to the throne of the United Kingdom of Great Britain and Northern Ireland.

In other words, a king-in-waiting.

The way he was raised owed much to an old black-and-white Pathé newsreel showing his grandmother and grandfather, the Queen and Prince Philip, returning to Britain in May 1954 after their long post-Coronation tour of the Commonwealth. On greeting her oldest son, then aged five, after an absence of six months, the new Queen shook his hand rather than hugging him.

That image was to have a lasting effect on William's mother, Diana, Princess of Wales. As she began to find her way inside the royal family, she resolved that her own children would never suffer such emotional remoteness. It set William's (and, later, Harry's) upbringing on a trajectory that fused, sometimes uncomfortably, the traditional royal stiff upper lip with behaviour that was informal, relaxed and approachable. Diana's hands-on mothering, given her position and workload, was in sharp relief to the way her husband, Prince Charles, had been raised by a succession of nannies. 'He's not hidden upstairs with the governess,' was her approach to William's upbringing. This yawning generational gulf was exposed early on when William's nanny was absent during a

Left: The Queen with her oldest son, Prince Charles, then aged five, on her return to London from her six-month tour of the Commonwealth, May 1954. The picture, from a Pathé newsreel, captures the formality of much of Charles's upbringing.

stay at Balmoral, the Queen's Highland retreat in Aberdeenshire. Diana took over the mothering herself, causing the Queen to exclaim, 'I don't understand why Diana has to do this. There are millions of housemaids around.'

The first sign of this change had come about by accident. In April 1983, some ten months after William's birth, the Prince and Princess were due to undertake a lengthy tour of Australia. As a royal novice, Diana was reconciled to leaving her son behind in England. However, an intervention by the Australian Prime Minister, Malcolm Fraser, inviting them to bring the baby along, transformed Diana's mood, affording her 'great fulfilment', but also signalling a break with the past, when royal children had invariably been left behind at Buckingham Palace while their parents were on tour.

She was always there to support, warn and encourage the young princes as they threaded their way towards understanding that they, particularly William, were not like other people. That one day he would be King.

This looming awareness of a special role in the world is a gradual process, as William's father recalled: 'I didn't just wake

up in my pram one day and say "Yippee!" I think it just dawns on you, slowly, that people are interested . . . and slowly you get the idea that you have a certain duty and responsibility.' Before William attended school, he genuinely had no idea that he was any different from anyone else. Although, as a youngster, he was the focus for occasional photo calls – he spent the whole time looking through the TV camera lens during one session in the garden at Kensington Palace – his mother told him that the photographers were only there to take her picture.

Perhaps William's first steps on the road to realization came when, in January 1987, aged four, he was enrolled at Wetherby School in Notting Hill. His innocence of his position was soon ended by fellow pupils, who left him in no doubt who he was. On one occasion a classmate reportedly asked him, 'Don't you know the Queen?' William looked at him and replied, 'Don't you mean Granny?'

Unsurprisingly, Harry was not slow to join the teasing of his older brother. When William said once that he would like to be a policeman and look after his mother, Harry told him emphatically: 'You can't, you have to be King.'

There were princely perks, however. On at least one occasion Diana took them to the police shooting range at Lippitts Hill in Essex where, under the watchful supervision of a police instructor, they learned to fire a .38 Smith and Wesson revolver.

Although William and Harry lived in a privileged world, a different world, it was not remote or aloof. That the boys went to exclusive private day schools close to their home was little different from many other children from well-to-do families living in Central London. Diana always made a point of taking them on the school run and of either picking them up herself when school ended for the day, or of being back from royal engagements in good time to be in the house when they came home.

Often they would sit with their mother in front of the TV eating beans or cheese on toast, or she would go into the kitchen and make something simple from scratch. Diana wanted William and Harry to be 'normal' as far as they were able within the bounds of their position and the constraints of security. 'She wanted her boys to experience life at first hand,' argues her hairdresser, Sam McKnight. 'One of her biggest goals was to learn from past mistakes in the family and have those boys buy a magazine in a shop, simple as that.'

It is a theme echoed by Ken Wharfe, her police protection officer: 'The children would have this interaction with normal people and it was a great education for them, frowned upon, I might add, by the Prince. In those early stages I don't think he'd liked what he would deem as familiarity. I think it was crucial to William and Harry for where they find themselves.'

The difference in parental approach to child rearing came into sharp relief when, on 3 June 1991, Prince William, then aged eight, was accidentally hit on the head with a golf club during practice at Ludgrove Preparatory School. He was taken to London's Great Ormond Street Hospital for Children, where he underwent an operation for a depressed fracture of the skull.

After establishing that his son was not in danger, Prince Charles continued with his official engagements, while Diana stayed with her son, leading to a slew of negative headlines about Charles's skills as a father.

The contrast with his wife could not have been more acute, especially when she began taking the boys, particularly William,

Right: Harry (left) and William, aged four and six respectively, playing on a vintage fire engine at Sandringham; the vehicle belongs to their grandmother, the Queen.

on visits to the other side of the social tracks, meeting the homeless, the lonely and the sick. She took him to visit terminally ill patients at the Royal Brompton Hospital, to a centre for the homeless, and to drop-in centres.

'I think she wanted him to realize at a very early age that there are other sides to life,' noted Sister Bridie Dowd of the Passage Day Centre, a shelter for the homeless in Central London that Diana and her older son visited. Shy at first, William ended up playing chess and talking about football. While some courtiers and members of the royal family, including her husband, disapproved of the egalitarian nature of the princes' upbringing, Diana was unrepentant. 'I want them to experience what most people already know – that they are growing up in a multi-racial society in which not everyone is rich, has four holidays a year, speaks standard English and has a Range Rover.'

Above: Diana with William at the Wimbledon Ladies' Final in June 1991. Everything in this shot speaks of the closeness between mother and son, at which Diana worked so hard.

Below: Diana on holiday in Mallorca, Spain, with William and Harry, August 1988. Diana was able to give them a relatively relaxed upbringing, despite the constraints placed upon the children of royalty.

The Princess had another agenda, however: an overarching scheme for which William, as he matured and began to realize the relentlessly constricting position that is the Head of State's, did not particularly thank her. Not only did Diana see herself as a Queen Mother for the twenty-first century, but she harboured a dream that, on the Queen's death, the throne would skip a generation and pass directly to her oldest son. 'If I were to write my own script,' she said in response to my question, posed in 1991, about her future, 'I would hope that my husband would go off with his lady [Camilla Parker Bowles] and leave me and the children to carry the Wales name until William ascends the throne. I'll be behind them all the way.' As far as William was concerned, though, the longer he could delay becoming King the better. He had a life to live without being hemmed in by the metaphorical prison walls of the Palace establishment.

Of course, Diana's dream was a reflection of the mistrust and hostility between her and Charles, the children used by both parties as pawns in a public-relations war.

A classic example was when, in March 1991, Diana decided to make a St David's Day visit to Cardiff, and thought that it would be a good idea to take William, then aged eight, for his first major royal engagement. Unwilling to allow his wife a publicity coup, Charles, who had other plans that day, abruptly changed his agenda so that he could join his son in Wales.

Diana's decision to bring William to Cardiff was, recalls her private secretary, Patrick Jephson, 'a powerful expression of her determination to play her part in teaching the young Prince her version of the art of kingship . . . Following his mother's gentle advice he squared his shoulders, determined to do what may be his lifetime's work. He was well up to the task.'

Above: 'He squared his shoulders, determined to do what may be his lifetime's work' – William with his mother during his first walkabout, Cardiff, 1 March 1991.

This parental rivalry continued behind the closed doors of Kensington Palace. William, sensitive and a little shy, was old enough to absorb the confusing emotional meaning behind the stony silences and harsh words when his parents were together. On at least one occasion he pushed tissues under the door to his mother's bathroom, where Diana had closeted herself so that the staff – and her children – would not see her crying. Another time, young Harry launched an attack on his father, ineffectually beating him on the legs with his fists and shouting 'I hate you, I hate you, you make Mummy cry . . . '

When Diana discussed the impending separation with the Queen, the boys' grandmother spoke for many when she told the Princess that the welfare of her grandchildren came first: 'My concern is only that those children have been the battleground of a marriage that has broken down.'

Shortly before the formal announcement, made by the then Prime Minister, John Major, in December 1992, Diana drove to Ludgrove, the prep school in Berkshire where William and Harry were boarders, to break the news. The boys' responses are instructive. Harry seemed bewildered and almost indifferent, while his older brother burst into tears. After he had composed himself, he told his mother, 'I hope you will both be happy now.'

Below: Separate lives? Princes William, Charles and Harry in a photograph taken at Highgrove for the Prince of Wales's Christmas card in 1995.

While the separation increased, rather than diminished, the haggling over the boys, probably the one thing on which both parents agreed was their attitude to journalism about them. In spite of the way that both manipulated the media, or tried to, each had an almost visceral contempt for the Fourth Estate. According to her police protection officer, Ken Wharfe, Diana repeatedly told her children that the press were 'bad, bad men'. Inevitably, the boys took their cue from their parents. During a holiday on Necker, the Caribbean island owned by British tycoon Richard Branson, the boys saw their chance to get their own back on the hated paparazzi. The brothers constructed two giant catapults between palm trees and launched a volley of water bombs – balloons filled with coloured water – against French paparazzi who were lying in wait in speedboats just offshore.

Above: Even after her official separation from Charles, Diana tried to maintain a cordial relationship with the royal family. She is seen here with the Queen at the wedding of the latter's nephew, Lord Linley, in October 1993.

18

They retreated after suffering several direct hits. As Wharfe recalled: 'For William, protecting his mother was a matter of personal pride and he rushed back to tell her of his victory, very much the hero in her eyes.'

This hostility towards the media, especially photographers, merely intensified with the passing of the years. During a skiing trip to Lech in Austria in March 1993, Wharfe became involved in an altercation with an Italian photographer who ended up on the ground outside the Arlberg Hotel where the royal party were staying. 'Do it again, Ken,' said a smiling Prince William. Diana had not seen the funny side, shouting 'Go away, go away!' at photographers. As Wharfe now reflects, that mountainside confrontation seems almost eerily prophetic in the light of what happened in the hours before Diana's death in Paris four years later.

Right: Skiing in Lech, Austria, in March 1993. The Princess's distaste for journalists and paparazzi is only too apparent; on this occasion, her police protection officer dealt summarily with an Italian photographer, to William's delight.

Left: Diana with Harry and William on holiday in the Virgin Islands in April 1990. For them, few holidays were free of the hated journalists and, worse, photographers.

For William, ever protective of his mother, this disrespectful behaviour, as he saw it, only fuelled his dislike of the media. As Diana's friend, Liz Tilberis, then editor of *Harper's Bazaar*, said, 'William understood her fury with them and he also understood that she courted them from time to time.'

The paparazzi, anonymous, disturbing but distant, were one thing. Much closer to home for William and Harry was the publication, in November 1994, of extracts from their father's authorized biography, written by the television broadcaster Jonathan Dimbleby. What concerned them most was the assertion that Prince Charles had been forced into marriage by their grandfather, Prince Philip, and that he had never loved their mother. It was yet another emotionally disorienting and disturbing episode for the two boys to absorb. When the book was first serialized in the *Sunday Times*, Prince Charles remained with the Queen Mother at her house on the Balmoral Estate, Birkhall. It was left to Diana to console her children, once again making the trip to their school in Berkshire. On the morning of 17 October 1994 she met her troubled children in the headmaster's study at Ludgrove. 'Is it true, Mother?' blurted out William. 'Is it true that Daddy never loved you?' She explained that when they had first married she and their father had loved each other as much as they now loved their children. It was an explanation of sorts. How far William, by then a bright twelve-year-old, accepted the explanation is another matter.

After all, just a few weeks earlier he had bought his mother a box of chocolates to console her after her lover, James Hewitt, had published his own story, *Princess In Love* (written with Anna Pasternak), in which he alluded to, though did not make explicit, the nature of their relationship. 'Mummy, I think you've been hurt. These are to make you smile again.'

Fiercely protective, he once boasted that he had put a photograph of the TV presenter Julia Carling on his dormitory wall and used it as a dart board after she had made disparaging and widely reported remarks about his mother, when it was revealed that Diana had become secretly entangled with her husband, the former England rugby captain Will Carling. 'She has picked the wrong couple this time,' Julia Carling told the media, a lightly veiled reference to the Princess's penchant for dalliances with married or unattainable men.

Although William was protective of his mother, as he moved into his teenage years he was becoming increasingly independent. As many mothers have discovered, he was at an age where his mother's presence on the touchline watching him play football or rugby was a source of embarrassment rather than pride. Both in private and in public, Diana was affectionate, tactile to a point where the Prince, clearly uncomfortable, would feign pushing her away. On one occasion he was clearly embarrassed when she made some admittedly light-hearted remarks about his performance on the school football pitch in front of his friends.

Yet if William was, in Diana words, 'her anchor', he was an anchor being dragged increasingly into his father's world, enjoying the time-honoured royal country pursuits of hunting, shooting and fishing. After graduating from learning the flora and fauna in the garden at Highgrove, his father taught him the art of fly fishing on the banks of the River Dee at Balmoral, and took the boys cubbing – hunting fox cubs – with a local hunt near his home in Gloucestershire.

Diana ruefully recognized the different path her boys were taking. Where once they had delighted in days out at an amusement park near London, now they much preferred the thrill of the chase. She made light of their love of country pursuits, calling the boys 'the Killer Wales'. 'All William wants to do is have a gun in his hand,' she remarked on one occasion.

William may have been a country boy at heart, but he was one with a difference. One day he would rule the country.

Right: The countryman Prince – one day to rule the country. William shooting at Sandringham in December 2004.

RECORDS AND WITNESSES

Below: The birth certificate for Catherine Elizabeth Middleton, registered at Reading in Berkshire in the month following her birth.

———•••———

Right: As his birth certificate shows, William is some five months younger than Kate. His father's profession is given as 'Prince of the United Kingdom', to Michel Middleton's 'Air Line Officer'.

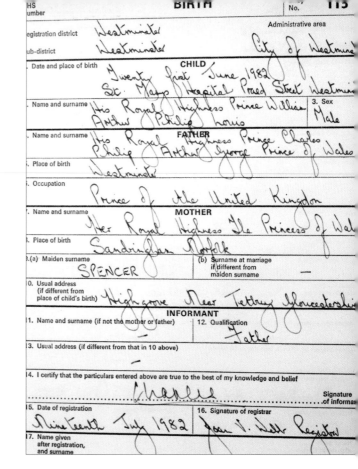

Top right: The marriage certificate for the then Princess Elizabeth and Prince Philip. The ceremony was held in Westminster Abbey, 20 November 1947.

———•••———

Centre right: The entry in the register at St Paul's Cathedral for the marriage of Prince Charles to Lady Diana Spencer, 29 July 1981.

———•••———

Bottom right: The marriage certificate for Michael and Carole Middleton. The wedding took place on 21 June 1980.

Marriage solemnized at _Westminster Abbey_ in the _Close_ of _St Peter Westminster_ in the County of _London_

When Married	Name and Surname.	Age.	Condition.	Rank or Profession.	Residence at the time of Marriage.	Father's Name and Surname.	Rank or Profession of Father.
20th November 1947	Philip Mountbatten	26	Bachelor	H.R.H. The Duke of Edinburgh K.G.	Kensington Palace	Andrew Henry Holstein Sonderbourg Glücksbourg (deceased)	H.R.H Prince Andrew of Greece
	Elizabeth Alexandra Mary Windsor	21	Spinster	Princess of the United Kingdom of Great Britain & Ireland	Buckingham Palace	Albert Frederick Arthur George Windsor	H.M. King George VI of the United Kingdom of Great Britain and Ireland and of the British Dominions beyond the Seas: Defender of the Faith

Westminster Abbey according to the Rites and Ceremonies of the _Established Church_ by _Special Licence_ by me

Philip
Elizabeth

in the presence of us:—

George R.   Marina
Elizabeth R.   Patricia Ramsay

Geoffrey Cantuar.
Alan C Don X
Edwin Richmond & Kirke
Mountbatten of Burma
Jacob B

1981

The Lady Diana Frances Spencer	20	Spinster	21		Althorp, Northampton	Edward John Spencer Earl Spencer	Peer of the Realm

Northern Ireland

Married in the Cathedral Church of St. Paul in London according to the Rites and Ceremonies of the Established Church by Special Licence of the Archbishop of Canterbury

By me   Robert Cantuar:

This Marriage was solemnized between us   Charles / Diana Spencer

In the presence of us   Elizabeth R   Philip / Elizabeth R

Edward   Andrew
Spencer   Frances Shand Kydd
Anne
Ruth Fermoy
Jane Armstrong-Jones

CERTIFIED COPY OF AN **ENTRY OF MARRIAGE**
Pursuant to the **Marriage Act 1949**
[Printed by the authority of the Registrar General.]

Registration District   Chiltern and Beaconsfield

840. Marriage solemnized at _St Paul's Church_ in the _Parish_ of _Dorney_ in the County of _Buckingham_

	When Married.	Name and Surname.	Age.	Condition.	Rank or Profession.	Residence at the Time of Marriage.	Father's Name and Surname.	Rank
3	21 Jan 1980	Michael Francis Middleton	30	Bachelor	Airline Officer	West View, Cock Lane, Bradfield, Berks	Peter Francis Middleton	R
		Carole Elizabeth Goldsmith	25	Spinster	Stewardess	20 Kingsbridge Rd, Norwood Green, Middx	Ronald John James Goldsmith	B

Married in the _Parish Church_ according to the Rites and Ceremonies of the _Church of England by Archbishop's Licence_ by me,   Paul Ham   Vicar

This Marriage was solemnized between us {   M.F. Middleton / C.E. Goldsmith   } in the Presence of us, {   R.Q. Holm / Peter F. Middleton   }

CATHERINE'S HERITAGE

*From Clarence Street
to Clarence House*

*H*ere was the village beauty, enraptured by the local squire, a rascally ladies' man by the name of William Corder. He wooed her, won her and, on bended knee, asked sweet Maria Marten to marry him. 'Yes, oh yes, dear William,' replied the lovestruck young woman.

It is unlikely that anyone watching the thirteen-year-old Kate Middleton utter those words on stage in an end-of-term play at her preparatory school could ever have imagined how prophetic they would prove. Kingsley Glover, who played the dastardly squire in the Victorian melodrama, *Murder in the Red Barn*, remembers his gangly teenage co-star as 'shy and skinny', a world away from the groomed, confident queen-in-waiting she is today.

Certainly the union of Kate Middleton and the very uncaddish Prince William has all the elements if not of a melodrama, then of a fairy tale. Catherine Middleton is the first commoner to marry a future monarch since 1660 when, on 30 September, the Duke of York and future King James II secretly wed his sister's pregnant maid of honour, Anne Hyde. Not since then has a prospective sovereign moved so far from the safe, if limited, haven of royalty and aristocracy. For Kate has but a pinprick of blue blood in her veins. The only ancestor she has in common with Prince William is Sir Thomas (later Lord) Fairfax, a leading Parliamentarian general during the English Civil War (1642–7), from whom William is descended through his mother's family, and Kate through her father's distant ancestors. Technically she and William are fifteenth cousins.

Although she talks in the clipped, plummy tones of Britain's upper classes and enjoyed an expensive private education, she hails from a family that is a snapshot of modern Britain, their history reflecting and refracting the tumultuous life of the nation. In less than a century they have journeyed from Clarence Street

in London's impoverished Southall to Clarence House, now the palatial London residence of Prince Charles and his consort, the Duchess of Cornwall, and the working office and apartment of Prince William.

Above: 'A princess of the people' – Kate at a rugby match in 2009.

The Middletons, as their name suggests (in Old English it originally described someone from the middle settlement), tell a story that goes to the heart of Britain, a tale of poverty, disease and premature death, of personal triumph, family tragedy and sacrifice for the common good. There are real-life villains, philanthropists, policemen, labourers, miners and lawyers, a family whose tangled roots spread all over the nation's compass and to farther shores. The future Queen can boast, albeit perhaps rather quietly, that her distant American relations, who live mainly in Williamsburg, Virginia, fought in both the War of Independence and the War of 1812 – but against the British King and his countrymen.

If William's mother was famously 'the people's princess', then Kate, or Catherine as she now wishes to be known, is truly 'a princess of the people'. Indeed, a good part of her family history is reminiscent of the 'upstairs-downstairs' melodrama in which

Below: Ronald and Dorothy Goldsmith, Carole Middleton's parents, in 1993. Mrs Goldsmith's 'airs and graces', and dreams of better things, earned her the family nickname 'Lady Dorothy'.

she starred during her schooldays. For more than a century her mother's ancestors, the Harrisons, worked as miners in the north-east of England, at one time employed in pits owned by the Bowes-Lyons, the family of Prince William's great-grandmother, the Queen Mother. Besides the daily hazards underground, generations of the Harrisons lived with grinding poverty and deadly disease, many members of the family dying prematurely.

It was not until after the end of the First World War, which claimed Kate's great-great-grandfather John, that a member of the Harrison family left the mines and learned a trade – Thomas Harrison, apprenticed as a carpenter. After the Second World War, he and his wife Elizabeth left their North-East roots and moved to a rundown house in Southall, West London. 'They came from nothing,' recalls their cousin Harry Jones. 'As poor as poor can be.' When, in August 1953, their eighteen-year-old daughter Dorothy, Kate's grandmother, married Ronald Goldsmith, it meant one less mouth to feed.

It was hardly as if Ronald, who was born in 1924 at 57 Clarence Street, Southall, one of the poorest streets in the neighbourhood, was the catch of the county. His family background was as hardscrabble as the Harrisons', his ancestors scraping a living as itinerant labourers, tradesmen, shopworkers and petty criminals – two relatives were transported to Australia in 1840 for stealing sheep. Living in insanitary conditions, the family was, like the Harrisons, blighted by early deaths, often from bronchitis.

For the first few years of their marriage Ronald, a lorry driver, baker and general handyman, and Dorothy, who worked as a shop assistant, lived with his mother in a condemned apartment in Southall. They may have been as poor as church mice, but when their first child, Carole, was born on 31 January 1955, Dorothy insisted on buying a huge Silver Cross pram – the Rolls-Royce of baby carriages – for her first-born. Known as 'Lady Dorothy' by her family for putting on airs and graces, Kate's grandmother was the driving force in the marriage. While Ronald was generally happy with his lot, Dorothy dreamed of a brighter tomorrow. In 1966, when Carole's brother Gary was born, they bought a new semi-detached house in Norwood Green, West London, where they stayed for the next twenty-five years. Carole, who attended local state schools, is remembered by her family as a typical 'girly' girl, trying on make-up, dancing to the *Top of the Pops* TV show and interested in fashion; as a teenager, she worked in a local fashion store every Saturday.

Carole Goldsmith's choice of career indicates that she had inherited some of her mother's ambition, for she won a coveted position as an air stewardess with British Airways (BA). 'British Airways was very exciting,' said former BA stewardess Shirley Keath (née Fogg). 'It was a wonderful career back then. There were always romances between pilots and stewardesses, but most of them didn't last.'

One romance that did stand the test of time, however, was between Carole and Michael Middleton, a dispatcher for British Airways, one of 130 managers responsible for ensuring the correct positioning and organization of the aircraft fleet. He had followed in the footsteps of his father Peter, a former RAF and commercial pilot who had once piloted Prince Philip. Unlike his new girlfriend's family, when the Middletons boarded a plane they instinctively turned left, at ease in the first-class world. Well-to-do and well-connected, for more than a century the Middleton family had turned out a successful lawyers in the northern city of Leeds. It was Noel Middleton who, in 1914, cemented the family's standing in the city when he married Olive, daughter of Alderman Francis Lupton, wealthy mill-owner and philanthropist who could trace his roots back to the Civil War Parliamentarian Sir Thomas Fairfax.

The inter-war years brought many changes to Britain, but Olive Middleton had the consolation of raising her family of three sons, Anthony, Christopher, and the youngest, Peter, born in 1920, who was Kate's grandfather. The boys were brought up in a stimulating artistic milieu, for their solicitor father, Noel, who was Chairman of the English Northern Philharmonia, held many musical soirées at his home. When the Second World War broke out in 1939, Peter's brothers Anthony and Christopher enlisted while Peter studied at New College, Oxford for a few months before joining the RAF Volunteer Reserve. He was posted to Canada as a flying instructor, first seeing action in August 1944 when he was posted to 605 Squadron at Manston, Kent. His task, which required skill and nerves of steel, was to fly his Mosquito fighter-bomber and try to tip the wings of German V-1 'doodlebug' flying bombs, so causing them to crash in open country, rather than falling on London. He later flew combat missions over France, Belgium and Germany.

The Middletons' first encounter with royalty came when Kate's grandfather, Peter, an airline pilot, was chosen for Prince Philip's lengthy tour of South America in 1962, flying a Britannia airliner. The Prince piloted many of the flights, usually with Peter by his side. Peter retired in May 1974 but, his adventurous spirit unquenched, he and his wife Valerie sailed across the Atlantic in August 1976 in their 35-foot ketch. Misfortune struck shortly after they had spent Christmas in the Caribbean, when they hit a reef off an island in the Bahamas. All they were able to grab before scrambling into their dinghy was a bottle of whisky and some ginger biscuits, which they put to good use when they landed on a deserted beach.

Left: Carole at a wedding in 1960, aged five; behind her is her paternal grandmother, Edith Goldsmith.

Above: Perhaps the sunny smile, neat turnout and good deportment foretold a career as an air stewardess – Carole aged five.

After he and his brothers were demobbed, Peter and his older brother Anthony met and eventually married twin sisters, Valerie and Mary Glassborow, daughters of a bank manager who had worked in Marseilles, in the South of France. The couples wed on 7 December 1946 and April 1947 respectively in an affluent Leeds suburb. Valerie gave birth to their first child, Richard, in September 1947, and their second, Michael – Kate's father – was born on 23 June 1949. In 1952 Peter Middleton joined British European Airways, the precursor to British Airways, and the family moved to Beaconsfield, Buckinghamshire, which was convenient for Heathrow (then called 'London Airport') and the River Thames, where he sailed with his sons.

After graduating from college in the early 1970s Michael followed in his father's footsteps, winning a place on the British Airways management-training scheme. He was subsequently appointed to a £35,000-a-year (US $56,000) position as one of the company's dispatchers.

He had a reputation as being pleasant and affable, as well as rather cautious – certainly in the eyes of his girlfriend. After he had been dating Carole Goldsmith for a few months they started living together in a house in Slough, west of Heathrow airport. The engagement ring came years later, once she had been proved airworthy – or rather, Middleton-worthy. In 1979, the

Above: Peter Middleton (second left) and his older brother, Christoper, at the former's marriage to Valerie Glassborow, December 1946. Valerie's twin, Mary (right), married Peter's brother Anthony a few months later.

Right: Kate's parents, Michael and Carole Middleton, at their home in Bucklebury. Years earlier, Michael had brushed off gossip with the remark, 'We are very amused at the thought of being in-laws to Prince William. But I don't think it is going to happen.'

year before their wedding, they paid £34,700, around £210,000 ($326,000) at today's prices, for a red-brick, semi-detached house in the ancient village of Bradfield Southend, Berkshire.

It took them eight months to knock their new home into shape, just in time for their wedding, which took place on 21 June 1980 at the Church of St James the Less in Dorney, Buckinghamshire. It was a glamorous affair, a small crowd of locals gathering to watch Carole, then aged twenty-five, and her father Ronald arrive for the service in a decorated horse-drawn carriage.

They had been married for less than a year when Carole fell pregnant, giving birth to her first child, Catherine Elizabeth Middleton, on 9 January 1982 at the Royal Berkshire Hospital in Reading. Shortly afterwards the dark-haired infant, dressed in a long white gown, was christened at the family's local church in Bradfield, St Andrew's. It was not long before they added to their family: Philippa Charlotte Middleton, known as Pippa, being born in September 1983 in the same hospital, and christened in the same church. Eight months later, in May 1984, the family moved to Amman in Jordan, to which Michael Middleton was posted by British Airways for two and a half years. Kate attended the Al-Saheera nursery school from the age of three, and could sing 'Happy Birthday' in Arabic before she could do so in English.

When they returned, Carole immersed herself in village life, taking her daughters to a playgroup at St Peter's Church Hall and later to nursery school. Naturally there were endless children's birthday parties, and at some point Carole hit on the idea of making up party bags commercially. At first she sold the bags locally, using her girls as models in her early catalogues, photographing them holding cupcakes.

As her business grew Carole never worried about help. Besides friendly and good-hearted neighbours, Carole's parents, Dorothy and Ronald, bought a home in nearby Pangbourne, while Michael's father and mother, Peter and Valerie, over the county border in Hampshire, were regular babysitters. Valerie, a

Left: Kate on the trampoline at her prep school in Berkshire; she was always good at sports.

Right: Carole Middleton out shopping with her older daughter. She and Kate remain very close.

nimble needleworker who embroidered country scenes, taught Kate – who, as a child, liked to be called Catherine – and Pippa the craft of sewing. Grandfather Peter, a skilled carpenter, made the children a pirate ship to play with in the garden and taught them how to sail on the Hamble estuary near his home in Hampshire. On these nautical excursions the youngsters responded to the commands of 'Captain Middleton' by crying out: 'Aye, aye, Kipper.'

Theirs was a rural idyll of 'Middle England'; a happy family life, fresh air, healthy country walks, playing dressing-up games – musical statues dressed as a clown was a favourite – and dancing with girlfriends, with Mum cooking something delicious in the kitchen. Kate's brother James, born in 1987, remembers playing with his sisters, sliding down the stairs on a tray, or sometimes baking cakes with their mother.

While their life may have been idyllic, it was one funded by hard work and commercial acumen. Carole Middleton's pin-money business grew apace, the busy entrepreneur soon having to rent premises on a nearby industrial estate. Called 'Party Pieces', her burgeoning enterprise supplied time-deprived yummy mummies with all they needed to make their children's parties

Left: Kate setting off for the gym from her parents' home at Bucklebury in July 2005. Once her relationship with Prince William was known photographers became a fact of life for her.

go with a swing. In the days before the Internet put everything a mouse-click away, her company supplied party essentials from hats to plates and gifts bags, all organized by Carole and her growing band of helpers. Like her mother, 'Lady Dorothy', Carole Middleton had the drive and dynamism to help secure her family's future.

Her friend and business colleague Lynda Tillotson recalls her overwhelming desire to succeed. 'She had to work hard to get where she is today … Carole might have been an air stewardess but she was a savvy girl. She is smart, works hard and has a steely determination.' In time, Carole's husband came to join the party, giving up his job at British Airways to help build the company.

In September 1989 he and Carole began to share the new school run, too, taking Kate to nearby Pangbourne, where she continued her education with 300 other boys and girls at St Andrew's, a fee-paying preparatory school whose motto is, perhaps appropriately in the light of events, 'We Seek Higher Things.'

Tall for her age, Kate excelled at swimming, netball, tennis – her grandmother, Valerie Middleton, was a keen tennis player, too – and broke the school record for the high jump. 'There wasn't a sport she couldn't turn her hand to,' recalls former classmate Samantha Garland. So it was natural that sporty Katie was one of the record crowd who, in spring 1991, went to watch the school hockey team play against their local rival, Ludgrove School, whose star attraction was Prince William, then aged nine. 'All the girls, Catherine included, were desperate to see him,' recalls a former pupil.

Early on, Kate showed a love of the limelight too, starring in school plays and pantomimes. It helped that she was tall, willowy and deemed by her contemporaries to be the prettiest girl in her year. Aged ten, she played Eliza Doolittle in *My Fair Lady*, the story of a young girl plucked from poverty and taught how to be a 'lady'. Her leading man, Andrew Alexander, remembers that Kate acted and sang with 'passion and conviction'. Now a professional singer, he recalls: 'I always like to think that although I'll never be king, I was at least her first prince.' In the school's production of *Murder in the Red Barn*, she told her lover, Squire William: 'I feel there is someone waiting to take me away into a life that's full, bright and alive.'

That bright new future was a new home, a flourishing family business and a new school. By April 1995 Party Pieces was doing sufficiently well to move to bigger premises, eventually employing eight full-time staff. A couple of months later, in July, the Middletons sold their three-bedroom house in Bradfield Southend for £158,000 ($253,000) and spent £250,000 ($400,000) on a five-bedroom detached home, Oak Acre, set in one and a half acres in the fashionable parish of Bucklebury.

Kate did not enjoy her new home for long, leaving in September that year for Downe House, an exclusive girls' boarding school in Thatcham, just five miles away. It was not a happy experience. She is remembered, according to writer Oliver Marre, as 'pale, quiet, shy, a little bullied'. Her friend and fellow

Above: 'A sporty outdoors girl' – Kate in the St Andrew's rounders team (rounders being a less elaborate and peculiarly British form of baseball).

pupil Emma Sayle recalls: 'Kate was not the most confident girl and it was always going to be tricky for her even though she was good at sports. Downe House is a great school but it is a fighting school. She was bullied.'

After two terms, her parents responded to her worries by taking her out of school. Significantly, Kate, who is now the most famous old girl, is not included on the list of Downe House alumni, which includes the writer Elizabeth Bowen, model Sophie Dahl and Prince and Princess Michael of Kent's daughter, Lady Gabriella Windsor.

Instead, her parents transferred her mid-term to one of the best-known private schools in Britain, Marlborough College, which had only fully opened its prestigious doors to girls in 1989. The £29,000-a-year ($46,500) boarding school in Wiltshire was originally founded in 1843 to educate the sons of poor clergy. Former pupils include the First World War writer Siegfried Sassoon and fellow poets Louis MacNeice and Sir John Betjeman.

As befitting a school steeped in literary history, Kate was immediately nicknamed 'Middlebum'; the senior boys, as apparently had become a tradition, holding up napkins in the school dining room where the new girl was marked out of ten. She did not score highly, according to contemporaries. If she had been unhappy at an all-girls school within jogging distance of home, then her treatment at the former boys-only school seems

Below: Kate (centre) with two of her friends at Marlborough College in Wiltshire, to which she went in the spring of 1996, having detested the two terms she had spent at the exclusive girls' boarding school Downe House.

even more disrespectful. Kate was assigned to Elmhurst House, one of three girls' boarding houses, where she lived with sixty-four others. Perhaps unsurprisingly she spent the first weeks quietly, retreating to her dorm after supper, gingerly testing the water, as it were, before diving in.

The arrival of girls in an essentially testosterone-fuelled environment meant that they had to learn to be tough. As another former pupil, the journalist Alice Thomson, recalls: 'You can't be precious or a perfectionist when you're on a cross-country run and a boy yanks your games skirt off for a dare. You just keep running.' Kate did survive, and seemed happy enough for her parents to send her sister Pippa to join her in 1997.

If the elder Middleton girl was reserved, she was also confident in herself, her judgement and her ability. As one of her tutors later recalled, she was good at 'mucking in'. 'She was dependable and loyal,' he says. Her genes from the Middleton

Above: At Marlborough, Kate excelled in several sports, notably tennis and, as here, hockey.

side of the family – lawyers who took an active interest in the arts – seemed prominent in her intellectual make-up. She was both methodical and artistic, good at maths and painting, and with a keen interest in photography, like her beloved grandfather, Peter Middleton. She continued to shine on the sports field, eventually becoming captain of the hockey team and playing first pair at tennis, which thrilled her doubles-playing grandmother, Valerie. A country girl at heart, when she was away from school, she went riding – even though she is allergic to horses – skiing, and sailing.

Of course, in the hothouse atmosphere of a co-educational boarding school, talk of boys was very much part of the daily conversational diet. For once 'Middlebum' lived up to her nickname. She and her friend Jessica Hay, who shared her dorm, would regularly moon at boys in the opposite house in a jolly game of 'guess the rear'. 'Our room faced out on to the boys' boarding house,' Jessica told the writer Elizabeth Sanderson. 'We'd take turns to show our bare bums to the guys to see if they could guess who they belonged to. Catherine kind of got addicted to it.'

In general, however, Kate had the reputation of being an observer rather than a participant, the girl who watched for the arrival of the house tutor while the other girls illicitly swigged vodka or smoked cigarettes. 'She didn't get involved in any drinking or smoking but was very sporty and family-minded,' added Jessica.

Her contemporaries remember that when it came to boys she followed a similar romantic trajectory to the late Diana, Princess of Wales. Just as Diana, to use her own euphemism, kept herself 'tidy' for what lay ahead, Kate seemed aloof to the charms of her male fellow pupils. As Jessica Hay recalled: 'We would sit around talking about all the boys at school we fancied but Catherine would always say: "I don't like any of them. They're all a bit rough." Then she would joke: "There's no one quite like Prince William."' According to contemporaries, however, her first boyfriend was fellow Marlburian Willem Marx, who is now a foreign correspondent.

As it was, she attended the kind of private school whose pupils often mixed with royalty as a matter of course. Not only was her friend Jessica Hay dating a scion of the Mountbatten clan, the Hon. Nicholas Knatchbull, but her fellow pupil Emilia d'Erlanger, a niece of the tenth Viscount Exmouth, was, in

August 1999, invited by Prince William on a ten-day cruise aboard a luxury yacht. While Emilia arrived back at Marlborough that summer with a tan, Kate, in her final year at the school, was a girl transformed. The seventeen-year-old duckling had turned into a svelte swan. 'It happened quite suddenly,' recalled Gemma Williamson. 'Catherine came back after the long summer break an absolute beauty. She never wore particularly fashionable or revealing clothes – just jeans and sweaters – [but] she had an innate sense of style.'

While at least one of her tutors has said dismissively that Kate was an 'unexceptional' student, she left the school, aged eighteen, with eleven GCSEs and three A levels in chemistry, biology and art, her grades good enough, then, to get her admitted into most universities.

As was the current fashion, she elected to take a year's break before making a final choice of where to study her preferred subject, History of Art. In September 2000 she enrolled in a three-month art and language course in Florence, Italy, steeping herself in the culture of the Renaissance, seeing at first hand the treasures she would study. She also undertook a programme for the Raleigh International charity in Chile, and was crew on a 'Round the World Challenge' boat in the Solent. 'She was hard-working and good fun,' recalled her skipper. 'She never mixed her romantic life with the sport, as I recall.'

That autumn she set her sails for her university of choice, heading north to St Andrews, an ancient seat of learning set in the seaside town on Scotland's east coast.

When she hauled her bags up the stone steps of St Salvator's Hall of Residence, Kate, in her jeans and Puffa jacket, looked like hundreds of other well-brought-up former boarding-school girls starting at university that autumn. Excited, if apprehensive, about what the future might hold, she was just another face in the crowd.

But not for long.

Right: Kate Middleton, no longer a princess-in-waiting, but a queen in the making.

WILLIAM

Turning a Corner

*I*n September 1995, when Prince William enrolled at Eton College, alma mater to the British Establishment, he was following a social trajectory that would have been entirely familiar to Queen Victoria. The school is a model of academic excellence, sporting achievement and effortless privilege, a place that has bred many Prime Ministers – including the present incumbent, David Cameron – and schooled countless young men of inherited fortune. Ironically, the elitist nature of this private educational establishment worked in William's favour – or that, at least, had been the thinking of both his parents. Diana, whose brother Charles had attended Eton, felt that the other boys, all high achievers in their own ways, would not be overawed by being in the presence of the future King and would therefore take him on his own merits. William too made light of his status. When he went to see the Queen for tea on a Sunday afternoon at Windsor Castle, close to Eton, a not infrequent occurrence, he would tell his friends that he was 'off to the WC'.

Well-mannered, sensitive and considerate, but instinctively suspicious – 'a deep thinker' was how his mother described him – there was, too, what might be termed a princely dimension to the young man, now thirteen, which was increasingly coming to the fore. William was becoming an assertive youth who knew his own mind and how to impose his will inside the Palace. As one former senior royal aide told me: 'Even when William was aged ten people were scared of him. He knew from a very early age that he could have what he wanted. Dealing with William getting his own way was a major part of the job.' This was more than just the sly skill of children who have learned to manipulate two warring parents to gain advantage for themselves. William's unique position as the future King gave him authority from an early age. He found himself living in a world where, with every passing year, fewer and fewer people would – or, indeed, could –

say 'No' to him. It has been the curse of princes down the ages, an endless and tantalizing vista of privilege and extravagance yoked to duty and obligation.

As Diana perceptively observed, the fact that William had a younger brother helped him share the burden, injecting levity into William's serious and sceptical view of a world that rested rather heavily on his slim shoulders. Those who watched both princes grow had remarkably similar views of their characters and their differences. Since the separation in 1992 they had seen William become more studious and distant, but increasingly aware of who he was and what he could do. He was both irritated and at times confused by the debate about his future path, and understandably troubled by the weight of the responsibility he would one day inherit.

Yet undeniably he has the Windsor stance, the Windsor temper and the Windsor manner. 'He acts a lot older than his years and these days I can see his father in him. That didn't use to be the case,' commented one courtier who has known William since he was a toddler. By contrast, Harry is very much a Spencer, with a remarkable resemblance to Diana's sister Sarah. He has the same quixotic recklessness, cheerfulness and uncomplicated love of life as many of those on that side of the family. 'Harry is like a Spencer – I don't have worries about him,' Diana told the designer Robert Devorik.

As William matured, his time at Eton also marked a transition in his relationship with his mother, for he found himself evolving into her chief adviser rather than needing her protection. As with many single parents without a partner to lean on, Diana's children, especially William, became her guides and comforters, even mentors. On one occasion the self-possessed teenager offered to make a speech for her when she admitted that she was nervous. 'Perhaps when you are older,' she said.

Yet as he became more independent, Diana increasingly confided in him, telling him details

Below: Diana, Princess of Wales in New York, three years after her separation. She had fewer worries about Harry than she did about his less outgoing older brother.

Above: In September 1994 Major James Hewitt, formerly of the Household Cavalry, published a book that alluded to his intimacy with Diana. Hewitt (second left) with William, Harry and their mother, to whom he was giving riding lessons. Diana later admitted the affair in her 1995 *Panorama* interview.

about her divorce negotiations and her boyfriends, confidences which, in an ideal world, William would not have wanted to hear. The Princess argued that it was better that her sons heard the truth from her rather than from exaggerated accounts in the media. The boys, who had learned from an early age to rely on one another, shared the burden of her confidences, often turning her confessions into light-hearted moments. While William was perplexed by her relationships, Harry joked about the men in her life, teasing her that she should hurry up and get married.

It was, however, the complicated web of relationships in her life that caused William the most concern. Before Diana's infamous TV interview in November 1995, during which she confessed her adultery with James Hewitt, and voiced her doubts about her estranged husband's suitability to be monarch, she took the trouble to visit William at Eton to try to explain why she had spoken in this way. A watching photographer captured the awkwardness of their exchange. William, it seemed, wanted nothing to do with his mother, his hurt plain and public.

The Princess's televised confession became all the more galling for William when it dawned on him that he and his brother had been dupes in her elaborate subterfuge. During the affair she had told the boys that Hewitt's presence at Highgrove was to help her overcome her fear of horses – she had broken her arm in a fall when she was a youngster – and to help improve their own riding skills. For some time after the broadcast her oldest son refused to speak to her. Unsurprisingly she later confessed that her one regret about the interview was that she had lifted the veil on her intimacy with Hewitt.

Diana and William had barely got back on to speaking terms when once again she behaved in a way that was both perplexing and painful. At the staff Christmas party in December she attacked the boys' irrepressible Girl Friday, Alexandra 'Tiggy' Legge-Bourke, who had been hired by Prince Charles to watch over them when they were in his care.

Diana had been indignant ever since Prince Charles had hired Tiggy, claiming that they were having an affair. If this was preposterous nonsense, worse was to follow. After Tiggy had visited her gynaecologist that summer, Diana concluded, wrongly that she had had a termination and that the baby had been fathered by Prince Charles. At the staff Christmas lunch she confronted Tiggy with a faux-sympathetic 'So sorry to hear about the baby.' The other woman nearly fainted at the vicious insult and had to be helped out of the gathering.

At that time Diana felt isolated, especially as she had just been informed of the formal request from both the Queen and Prince Charles to finalize the divorce. Yet while this unwelcome news may have explained her behaviour, it did not excuse it. Significantly, Tiggy remains a good friend of both William and Harry.

Above: William with Tiggy Legge-Bourke, the 'irrepressible Girl Friday' whom Prince Charles had engaged to look after his sons when they were with him.

As she wrestled with her newly single status, it was her older son who helped her write the first page of a new chapter in her life. Early in 1996 they had been looking at her clothes at Kensington Palace. Seeing them, William suggested that she sell her gowns for charity as a way of saying farewell to her old life. It was an inspired idea, in keeping with her desire to free herself from the shadow of her past. The auction, at Christie's in New York in July that year, raised $5.7 million (£3.5m) for cancer and AIDS charities.

Serious beyond his years, William was the one man close to her whom Diana could have trusted never to betray her or let her down. Ironically, their last conversation was a mixture of parental distance and intimacy. While Diana lay on the deck of a luxury yacht under the Mediterranean sun – courtesy of her latest boyfriend, Dodi Fayed – William was concerned about an edict from Buckingham Palace that he had to attend a photo call to mark his third year at Eton. It was part of what he considered a Faustian bargain made with the media – he would be left alone to continue his schooling in peace in return for occasional access.

Right: Diana at the auction of her gowns at Christie's, New York, in July 1996, just before her divorce. William had provided both the idea and the impetus for the sale as a way of casting off her old life; the auction raised millions for charity.

The problem, as he told his mother in that last call, was that Harry had been kept back a year at Ludgrove, so the focus of the press was bound to be on his underachievement at school, rather than on William's steady academic progress. Diana promised to discuss the matter with his father next day, when she arrived home after a night in Paris with Dodi. She never returned, being fatally injured in the Place de l'Alma tunnel in Paris after her chauffeur-driven Mercedes smashed into a concrete pillar, killing Dodi Fayed and the drunk driver, Henri Paul, and badly injuring their bodyguard, Trevor Rees-Jones.

At Balmoral, a world away from the baying paparazzi and the bright lights, Prince Charles braced himself to tell William and Harry the terrible news, the immediate consensus being that the boys should be left to sleep through the night. In the morning, as William began to absorb the full import of what had occurred, he said that he had thought something awful had happened as he had kept waking up during the night.

Numb with shock, they attended the traditional Sunday service at nearby Crathie church, during which Diana's name was not mentioned once, prompting Prince Harry to wonder whether his mother really was dead. So began the most turbulent week for the royal family since the abdication of Edward VIII in 1936, a

Above: July 1997: Diana with her last lover, Dodi Fayed, at St-Tropez in the South of France, just weeks before they were killed in a car crash in Paris.

week in which the Queen's response to Diana's death, and that of the rest of the royal family, were sharply criticized by media and public alike.

One of the most difficult decisions, as the then Prime Minister, Tony Blair, was later to reveal, was whether the boys should walk behind the gun-carriage bearing their mother's coffin in the funeral procession, in keeping with royal tradition. At the most traumatic moment in their lives, the young princes once again found themselves used as emotional shuttlecocks, flying between warring factions inside the royal family and between the Spencers and the Windsors. Diana's brother, Charles, Earl Spencer, objected to the boys walking behind her coffin on the grounds that she would not have wanted her children to go through so painful an ordeal. 'I thought that was where tradition and duty went too far against human nature,' he said later. While the final decision was left up to the boys, it was the intervention of their grandfather, Prince Philip, that proved crucial. 'If I walk, will you walk?' he asked. William agreed. Significantly, they walked for their grandfather, not their father or uncle.

Right: William, Harry and their father looking at tributes to Diana left by the public outside the gates of Balmoral, a few days after her death.

Left: Prince Philip, Prince William, Earl Spencer, Prince Harry and Prince Charles follow the gun carriage bearing Diana's coffin in the procession to Westminster Abbey on 6 September 1997.

In a week redolent with symbolism, their decision to join the procession to the abbey was probably the most telling, the sight of the two young princes walking behind their mother's coffin a potent and enduring image of loss and grief. As Charles Spencer recalled: 'That walk was just a nightmare. The worst experience of my life was walking behind my sister's body to Westminster Abbey. Worrying about the boys and thinking, this is so horrendous and so public.'

Paradoxically, it was the fact that the boys displayed the traditional royal virtues of stoicism and fortitude amidst a sea of public grief that lent the tableau such an emotional resonance. As Prince Harry later told Matt Lauer, presenter of NBC's *The Today Show*: 'If we don't feel comfortable pouring our eyes out in front of thousands of people, then that's our problem. You know, we have got each other to talk to.'

As the months passed this loathing of the media ate away at the boys, William proving especially unbending in his hatred. At one point he even talked about becoming a recluse. Even as evidence mounted that the paparazzi had been nowhere near at the time of the accident and that the awful banality of a drunk driver had caused his mother's death, he remained implacable.

It was a serious problem for the Palace. Gently wooing William back into the royal fold, rehabilitating Charles's battered image and winning public acceptance for Camilla was the dauntingly difficult challenge facing courtiers.

The scale of the task, particularly with regard to corralling William, was underlined during a visit to Vancouver with his father and brother in March 1998. On arrival, the fifteen-year-old prince was visibly overwhelmed by 'Willsmania' as thousands of well-wishers, mainly young girls, waited to greet him. It seemed that 'His Royal Shyness', as the local Canadian media dubbed him, would rather be back in his rooms at Eton than undergoing ordeal by screaming fans.

Below: William on walkabout in Vancouver in March 1998; he was visibly overwhelmed by 'Willsmania', and was dubbed 'His Royal Shyness' by the Canadian media.

More significantly, William quickly rearranged the royal schedule, banning the media from a space centre that he and Harry intended to visit the next day. It was a rude awakening for William, the Canadian visit being one of the first times he had been out and about in public since his mother's death. As he later admitted to Matt Lauer, he felt vulnerable: 'Wherever you went, people were watching you, just because, you know, they were interested to see how you react or what you're thinking because of that [Diana's death]. And that was quite hard.'

However, he did agree, albeit grudgingly, to an interview for his sixteenth birthday in June 1998. In answer to a series of innocuous written questions, the Prince revealed that he planned to study biology, geography and history of art for his A levels, that he enjoyed being at Eton but that, unsurprisingly, he did not enjoy the spotlight.

Left: In the aftermath of Diana's death, Prince Charles's staff achieved a near-miracle: the rehabilitation of Charles and his long-time mistress, Camilla Parker Bowles (seen here with the Queen at Highgrove), in the public consciousness.

Above: Camilla, Duchess of Cornwall, as she had become following her marriage to Prince Charles, with William (in RAF uniform) at a service at St Paul's Cathedral in October 2009.

While William instinctively wanted to be left alone, Camilla deliberately kept a low profile, as courtiers carefully introduced her to the wider world. Prince William was, as Diana's former private secretary Patrick Jephson points out, effectively used as her 'human shield', information about the young prince being given out in return for favourable coverage of Charles and Camilla.

The pivotal moment was the first meeting between William, whose looks and manner made him the living embodiment of the dead Princess, and her arch-rival, Charles's mistress. This encounter finally took place a few days before his sixteenth birthday, on Friday, 12 June, at St James's Palace. He had just been going out to the cinema with friends when his father asked if he wished to meet the woman who was now a permanent fixture in his, Charles's, life. William agreed, the two of them chatting for thirty minutes before he went on his way. Afterwards Camilla, or so selected correspondents were helpfully told, needed a stiff vodka-and-tonic.

A few weeks later it was leaked that William had been instrumental in inviting Camilla to join the royal party on a Mediterranean cruise in August. The signs were clear. The young Prince's presence in Camilla's company was forgiveness for perceived past transgressions, a kind of latter-day version of the royal laying-on of hands. For the watching media and the public, the subtext was obvious: if William could forgive, so could the rest of the world.

Yet though he might be able to forgive, he could not forget. At Balmoral that summer, he joined the Queen and the rest of the royal family, as well as Tony Blair, for a service in Crathie church to mark the anniversary of Diana's death. The Prime Minister, who had captured the public mood when he had spoken of Diana as 'the people's princess', talked with William, who was still grieving and angry, furious at the conflict between public position and private emotion that he had endured in the week leading up to his mother's funeral.

As Blair astutely observed in his autobiography: 'He knew now, if he didn't before, what being a prince and a king meant. For all the sense of duty, the prison walls of hereditary tradition

Right: William at Eton: looking typically wary, especially of any camera (left); playing in a school football game (right); and 'attempting to cook' (below). In his last year at the school he brushed off written questions from the press about his future.

Left: 'Almost the only peace William could find was among his friends at Eton' – William and Harry with William van Cutsem and Tiggy Legge-Bourke.

must have seemed too high a price to pay.' No matter how high they built these walls, the princes could not escape the endless speculation surrounding their mother's death, conjecture fuelled by Mohammed Fayed's absurd and distasteful insistence that their grandfather, the Duke of Edinburgh, had masterminded her and Dodi's assassination. Days after the anniversary of Diana's death, her sons issued a plea asking the public to let their mother rest in peace.

Almost the only peace William could find was among his friends at Eton, who respected his need for privacy. During his senior years he became a member of Pop, was made Captain of Swimming and joined the Army section of the school's Combined Cadet Force, ultimately winning the prestigious Sword of Honour. As a component of his studies in the history of art, he worked in the military-medal section of Spink and Co., part of Christie's auction house, and, as part of his geography field studies, inspected at close quarters the inhabitants of a run-down inner-city London estate notorious for drug-related crime.

As fascinating as such exotic, if dangerous, species might be, William was interested in varieties much further afield. He acquired a taste for life beyond Britain's shores during his summer vacation in 1998, when he visited the 55,000-acre game reserve owned by Ian and Jane Craig in the magnificent Lewa Downs, overlooked by Mount Kenya. 'William just loves Africa, that's clear,' Ian Craig reflected afterwards. 'He did everything from rhino spotting to anti-poaching patrols to checking fences.' He learnt the rudiments of Swahili and in time became involved in the Tusk Trust, a conservation charity founded by the Craigs, whom he considered his 'second family'. Of course, the fact that they had a beautiful daughter, Jecca, sparked media interest. One published story that they had secretly become engaged was dismissed by Clarence House, on William's authority, as fanciful.

His real love affair, in fact, was with Africa, one which he was to renew again and again, beginning with a safari holiday to Botswana with his brother and Tiggy Legge-Bourke in the spring of 1999. The continent spoke to him, as it does to so many who

Below: William regarded the time he took off after leaving Eton as his 'year as an "ordinary guy", anonymous and normal,' which he found refreshing. Here, in Chile, he relaxes on his bunk during a quieter moment.

visit it, the Prince planning his gap year around a fourteen-week safari that included visits to South Africa and Botswana, a trip down the River Nile and, of course, time on the Craigs' reserve in Kenya. While William had mischievously suggested that he wanted to spend his time before going up to university playing polo in Argentina, he was sensible enough to realize that his year out of the limelight had to have princely point and purpose, combining worthwhile projects with strenuous outdoor pursuits. As was now a familiar part of William's life, akin to Hollywood film stars discussing their lives to promote their latest movies, for his eighteenth birthday he posed for a series of pictures inside Eton itself – shots of him playing water polo and attempting to cook, among others – and stonewalled written questions about his future plans.

Once he finished his last term at Eton, he flew to Belize in Central America, where he joined the Welsh Guards on 'Exercise Native Trail', during which he learned jungle survival techniques. He returned briefly to Highgrove for a media reception, in the course of which he answered questions about life as a young adult. This was in exchange for the media's undertaking to leave him alone during his gap year. Psychologically, he seemed to have turned a corner, for the resulting press coverage deemed him to be personable, confident and gracious, although he uttered his now familiar refrain about being uncomfortable in the limelight. He preferred to focus on the joys of a life less extraordinary, explaining that he had raised around £5,000 ($8,000) via a sponsored water-polo match he had organized to fund his main trip, this time to Chile as a volunteer for the Raleigh International charity. During the ten-week visit to Patagonia, one of the most remote places on the planet, he went kayaking and spent weeks tracking and monitoring the huemul, an indigenous but endangered species of deer.

Ironically, it was his time back in Britain working as a lowly farmhand on a dairy farm, milking the herd of cows at four in the morning before mucking out, which was the highlight of his year as an 'ordinary guy', anonymous and normal. 'I got my hands dirty, did all the chores,' he remarked. Then, after an amazing trip around Africa, he was ready to get his hands dirty again, at least academically speaking, as he prepared for his next big adventure – university.

Right: On his way to repair walkways in the village of Tortel, during his time in Chile as a volunteer for the charity Raleigh International.

WILLIAM

The Student Prince

He might have been the talk of town and gown, but the last thing Prince William was looking for was attention – or love, for that matter – when he first arrived at Scotland's oldest university, St Andrews, in the autumn of 2001.

While he may have allowed himself a wry smile at reports of American mothers driving their student daughters to the seaside town in Fife, on Scotland's east coast, famous as the cradle of golf, he had other matters on his mind. Yet again the young prince was at the centre of a royal tug-of-war, this time between his father and his uncle, Prince Edward.

Since Diana's death in 1997, Britain's mass media had agreed a protocol to allow her sons to grow up in relative privacy in return, again by agreement, for occasional picture opportunities and interviews. Before William arrived at his new university, Prince Charles and his son had kept their side of this 'gentleman's agreement', allowing the media to follow them around Scotland during a day's royal duties, after which the press withdrew to let him pursue his dream of being just 'a normal student'.

Everyone left – everyone, that is, except representatives of his uncle Edward's television company, Ardent Productions, who continued to follow William around St Andrews. Prince Charles was so incensed by his youngest brother's behaviour, or rather the behaviour of his employees, that he contacted him, demanding an apology. The then Rector of St Andrews, the broadcaster and journalist Andrew Neil, was flabbergasted by Prince Edward's attitude. 'You just couldn't make it up,' the canny former newspaperman recalled.

For William though, this world of make-believe was his daily reality. Since babyhood, everyone, inside and outside the royal family, had wanted a piece of him. As the future King he was a living icon. It was a fact of his life that he had struggled to get used to. In his mind he came with more baggage than the

average camel train. What girl would truly be interested in him when they glimpsed the weight of expectation – and history – resting on his young shoulders? 'Why would anyone want to go out with me?' he once confided.

No sooner had he arrived than he had to cope, somewhat bashfully, with a crowd of around two thousand well-wishers, mainly townsfolk and tourists, waiting to greet the Prince and his father. It was a brief public encounter, the nineteen-year-old eager to be installed in his new lodging, room B31 on the second floor of St Salvator's Hall of Residence, where he would live for the first year of the four he would spend studying History of Art at St Andrews. 'I felt kinda sorry for him,' said fellow undergraduate Allie Giddings, an American student who had watched his arrival from the back of the enthusiastic crowd.

Not as sorry as he felt for himself. William's reluctance to be paraded around the east-coast town like a trick pony was understandable, for he had made it clear in an interview before arriving that he wanted to be treated like a normal person. 'I just want to go to university and have fun,' he declared. 'I want to go there and be an ordinary student.' Albeit an ordinary student who had arrived late because of a jolly lunch he had enjoyed with the Queen Mother at her Highland home, Birkhall on the Balmoral Estate. Herself the holder of an honorary degree from St Andrews, her parting words to her great-grandson were, 'Any good parties, invite me down.'

With the barely disguised exasperation of a young man who has just returned to the unwanted limelight after a gap year travelling the world largely unnoticed and anonymous, the teenage Prince observed: 'I mean, I'm only going to university. It's not like I'm getting married – although that's what it feels like sometimes.' In fact, as his father had discovered before him, his decision to attend university was indeed something of an arranged marriage, whether he liked it or not. It had not been his choice alone.

As with marriage, there had been many factors to take into consideration when choosing the university he would attend. Not only would his four-year stint in Scotland give the future King a chance to learn more about the country over which he would one day reign, but life would be made much more difficult for the paparazzi, who regularly dogged his footsteps when he was in London.

Given that privacy and security ranked highly in official and personal thinking, academic priorities came some way down the list when it came to making a decision, though William's A-level grades meant that he met the admission standards for his course. While his final choice was strongly influenced by his Eton housemaster Dr Andrew Gailey, he was as attracted to the countryside as the academic course. As he cogently explained about his choice of university, 'There is plenty of space, I love the hills and mountains and thought St Andrews had a real community feel to it. Somewhere like Edinburgh is just too big and busy for me.'

Below: 'He had to cope, somewhat bashfully, with a crowd of around two thousand well-wishers . . . waiting to greet the Prince and his father.'

William's love of Scotland was partly inspired by time spent at Balmoral, but also by holidays at the home of the woman he called 'Granny Frances', Diana's mother Frances Shand Kydd, on the remote island of Seil, on the west coast of Scotland. He fondly remembers an idyllic week in August 1989 when he and his younger brother were able to roam freely around the island.

With Balmoral a two-hour drive from St Andrews, William had a ready-made bolthole should student life begin to grate. His father had enjoyed a similar option during his years at Cambridge. Most weekends, especially during the shooting season, he had headed to the Queen's 20,000-acre Norfolk estate at Sandringham, to escape the lonely confines of his university room. A shy, rather sensitive young man, Charles had struggled to make contact with his fellow students, as he also had during his schooldays at Gordonstoun, a private boarding school in the remote north-east of Scotland. He later described the school as 'Colditz in kilts', and some of his fellow pupils as 'foul'.

At Cambridge, he endured a different kind of exile within the student community, as his biographer and friend Jonathan Dimbleby explained: 'Chronically self-conscious, he found communal gatherings in the absence of "his cronies" acutely embarrassing; there would always be a space around him caused by a peculiar reluctance to engage the Prince of Wales

Above: The North Sea coast at St Andrews can provide good surfing, as William discovered during his time there. However, the town lies further north than Moscow, so a wet suit is often a necessity.

in conversation, to stand by him in a queue or take the empty seat at his side. If he wanted to communicate across that void between the monarchy and its subjects he had always to make the first move, but to make contact with his fellow undergraduates required an effort of will that he could not yet achieve.' Like a mole daring the sunlight, Charles was tentative in his dealings with the outside world. According to one of his circle, 'He was unbelievably strait-laced, very much reserved and never let down his guard.'

While William's temperament differed markedly from his father's – he was and is much more worldly-wise – he was equally suspicious of outsiders. It is a reflex he learned from an early age. When callers telephoned Diana at Kensington Palace they were often surprised to hear a rather solemn young voice answer. The schoolboy Prince William was serious and unfailingly courteous, but gave nothing away to those whose voices he did not recognize.

Schooled in suspicion, trusting few and often putting newcomers to an unspoken test of discretion and allegiance, William had a finely tuned nose trained to sniff out sycophants and social climbers. 'People who try to take advantage of me and get a piece of me – I spot it quickly and soon go off them.' While

Below: Some of the best holidays William and Harry spent were with 'Granny Frances', Diana's mother, Frances Shand Kydd, at her home on a remote Scottish island. Diana with Harry, William (foreground, in blue) and her mother (far right) in 1992.

he recognized, like his father, that his position was imbued with as much social stigma as status, setting him apart from the herd, he adopted a pragmatic approach. So, for example, he studiously avoided joining the new intake of St Andrews students at Freshers' Week, during which many newly arrived undergraduates ('freshmen') drink too much and make fools of themselves. Not only was he aware that media interest in him might overshadow the boozed-up behaviour of other freshmen but, as he told writer Sam Greenhill: 'I thought I would probably end up in a gutter completely wrecked and the people I had met that week wouldn't end up being my friends anyway.'

Among his small circle of friends were several Old Etonians, including lawyer's son Fergus Boyd and Olli Chadwyck-Healey, as well as others in a group known as 'Sally's Boys', after their hall of residence, St Salvator's. They included Ali Coutts-Wood, Graham Booth, Charlie Nelson and Oli Baker. In an idiosyncratic tradition, a freshman like William Wales, as he termed himself, were taken under the wing of older academic 'parents' to help ease them into university life. His 'father' was Old Etonian Gus McMyn, while his 'mother' was an American from Connecticut, Alice Drummond-Hay, a childhood friend of the Prince and a granddaughter of the Earl of Crawford and Balcarres.

William may have missed Freshers' Week, but he did not escape another rite of passage – a nickname accorded by his peers, becoming known by one and all in his college lodgings as 'P. Willy'. That jaunty epithet, however, disguised the sober fact that, like his father, he was different, a 24-carat celebrity, a megastar in the university firmament. His arrival at Ma Bells, his favourite local pub, or in the student common room or the St Salvator's dining room, would provoke a range of reactions from others, from the gauche to the indifferently hostile.

Ana Fernatt, a student from Chicago, described her own behaviour when she 'bumped into' the future King while standing in line for lunch. Ana, who boasted that she had seen him wearing nothing but a towel on three occasions in the hall of residence, shook his hand, introduced herself and then asked him what his name was. As she later advised: 'Never ever do this. You will look like a weirdo. Also, if you see him sitting by himself you do not need to go sit next to him and continue the awkward exchange you started.'

William had a wide circle of friends at St Andrews, among them Ali Coutts-Wood (left), with fellow undergraduate Meghann Gunderman from Charlotte, North Carolina; Fergus Boyd (right), also with Ms Gunderman; and Oli Baker (below).

Left: St Andrews days – William replacing his socks after running through the tide along the wide, sandy beach.

Many considered it seriously 'uncool' even to mention the Prince in conversation with fellow students. As Neil Holmes Walker, who started at St Andrews in 1999, recalled, 'Any comment about him implies that his presence affected your decision to study here, making you a fan and a social climber. Nothing could be worse than to be thought of as keen to meet William.' Even the idea of saying 'Hi' at a party or in a pub was considered 'social suicide'. This endless mutual wariness between crown and gown made for a lonely life, as William once admitted.

Much as he wanted to be normal, to be one of the boys, even that was fraught with difficulties. When Michael Choong, as captain of one of the university's rugby teams, persuaded William to 'get his shorts dirty', he never imagined the repercussions. While the Prince was a lucky mascot – his team never lost when he turned out on the wing or at centre – the opposition invariably singled him out for rough play. On one occasion he was hit so hard in a tackle that his captain asked if he wanted to leave the pitch for treatment for a painful neck injury. 'He really took some stick,' recalls Choong. 'He never grumbled and always came back for more. He could take it and dish it out. Wills wasn't as skilful or talented as he thought he was but he was super-fit, a real workhorse and never knew when he was beaten.'

It was little different when he played his preferred sport, water polo, a game he had taken up while at Eton. The six-man team game is brutal and robust, and tactically, players try to intimidate their opponents by grabbing their private parts.

Clearly the chance to smash and grab the 'crown jewels' was an enticing prospect for many of William's opponents – and a painful one for the Prince. As American college water-polo

Right: William (player at left) during a rugby game at St Andrews. His team captain recalled: 'He really took some stick. He never grumbled, and always came back for more. He could take it and dish it out.'

player Matt May observes: 'The grabbing of an opponent's testicles is … a tactic that is prevalent in college polo upwards. Even at Olympic level.' None the less, William was elected captain of the university's water-polo team, going on to be chosen to play for the Scottish National Universities side in the annual Celtic Nations sports event, in which, ironically enough, his team lost 15–6 to Wales.

Along with weekly two-hour training sessions in a hotel swimming pool, William took morning rides astride a yellow rubber inflatable banana in the freezing North Sea and cycled around the town, although he also enjoyed a quiet game of pool in a local pub.

Not that the pub would remain quiet for long. It became a standing joke among his group of friends that within minutes of his sitting down for a quiet pint of cider the place would quickly fill up with female students. On one occasion a female undergraduate, clearly the worse for drink, lurched over to him in the bar and shook his hand, before promptly throwing up. Another time an American student marched up to him at a fancy-dress dinner and boldly introduced herself. He grinned, grabbed her elaborate hat and skimmed it across the dance floor. 'He was not being nasty, just flip,' recalled a contemporary. 'She was surprised, but he meant no harm by it.' Not that William was himself immune to celebrity. He was awestruck when he spotted the former England football striker and TV pundit Alan Shearer in a local bar and quickly dispatched his bodyguard to effect an introduction.

He was very much onside as the main attraction on campus, a male pin-up watched, if not wooed, by an assiduous fan club. The buzz had started the moment he announced his decision to attend the university. Girls, particularly those who had been to private schools like Marlborough, talked about applying to St Andrews as much for the social cachet of being able to say that they were studying at Prince William's university, as for any

Above: Water polo is a brutal and robust game, but even so William ended up as captain of the university's team.

fanciful notion that they might possibly date the future King. It was a form of social one-upmanship among the middle classes with daughters of university age, similar to when Princess Anne's son Peter Phillips had attended Exeter University in the West Country a couple of years earlier.

In his first term, the Prince found this attention as unwanted as it was wearing. 'He got fed up with people who would do anything to meet him,' recalls Michael Choong, a member of the Freshman Committee. 'Some American girls were so desperate to be around William that they literally followed him by enrolling into the History of Art course. Will hated that kind of stuff but he learned to live with it.'

As an alpha male, he preferred to be the predator rather than the quarry, he and his friends rating girls they spotted in the college dining room, or celebrities they fancied as they leafed through glossy magazines. 'She's hot,' was William's oft-used phrase. He was known for his roving eye, which would cast around a room checking out the female talent, while he appeared to be absorbed in his companion's conversation. As a member of

Below: William enjoying a quiet game of pool in a St Andrews pub during his last year at the university. The pub would rarely stay quiet for long, once word of his presence reached the ears of eager female undergraduates.

Left: 'She's hot' was an expression the young Prince used frequently, and he was known for his roving eye where female 'talent' was concerned.

Right: William, probably sensibly, declined to join the traditional raucous celebrations of Raisin Week at the end of his first term at St Andrews. He therefore missed the sight of his fellow History of Art student, 'Beautiful Kate', covered in foam.

his circle told me: 'Everyone thinks Harry is the naughty one. Not true. William is a ladies' man.'

He was little different from his contemporaries in sizing up desirable members of the opposite sex. One of the hottest topics of conversation in the St Salvator's dining room during the first term was a certain Kate Middleton, also known as 'Beautiful Kate'. In the febrile, hothouse college atmosphere she had a number of admirers. As Michael Choong recalls: 'Guys would go to the canteen for breakfast and they would eye up Kate. They'd be joking: "Who's going to date Kate?" Then someone would turn to Will and remark: "Obviously, you've got the best chance."'

And yet the conventional divide between idly ogling a student and actually talking to a girl he liked was wider for William than for his student posse. Royal romance was fraught with difficulties. Not only was there the ever-present danger of

a girlfriend – or a member of her circle – selling her story but, more likely, any budding romance would be curtailed once the media discovered the girl's identity. William was as concerned for their privacy – and that of their families – as anything else. As he observed: 'These poor girls. They suddenly get thrown into the limelight and their parents get rung up and so on. I think it's a little unfair on them, really. I'm used to it, but it's very difficult for them and I don't like that at all.'

During his first term he became friendly with several girls, including Carley Massy-Birch, a second-year English student whom he met when he auditioned for the role of Zooey in a play based on *Franny and Zooey* by the American novelist J. D. Salinger. Although successful in the audition he was not given the role, the producer telling him that he was worried that the media, rather than townsfolk and fellow students, would dominate the audience in the small Byre Theatre during the four-night run. The rejection symbolized for William the frustrations of fitting into university life.

However hard he tried, he could not be just an 'ordinary student'. Towards the end of his first term in November, for example, as much as he wanted to join in the traditional raucous celebrations of Raisin Week, when students parade through the town in fancy dress before being sprayed with shaving foam and other liquids in the college quad, he prudently decided to stay away. He missed the sight of his fellow History of Art student, 'Beautiful Kate', covered in foam and downing vodka shots and dirty mixed drinks as one of a breakfast party of boozy hockey and rugby players. She politely declined to join several of the boys who stripped off and streaked down the street.

At the end of the first term, however, wine and rosy romance were the last things on William's mind. His sense of exclusion and his weariness of being treated like a specimen on a petri dish, scrutinized, prodded and poked by all and sundry, gave him second thoughts about continuing at university. After the relative obscurity of his gap year, normal day-to-day student life at St Andrews had come as too much of a shock to the royal system. He told his father that he wanted to leave. 'He was sick of people he didn't know following him around. He was ready to call it a day,' says Michael Choong.

Prince Charles, recalling his own difficulties in settling to university life, was understanding but left it to others, as is his wont, to convince his son to stay on. Prominent among the voices encouraging the latter to continue at St Andrews but perhaps change courses was his former housemaster at Eton, Dr Andrew Gailey. Since several of William's friends were taking Geography, his favourite and strongest subject academically, he was persuaded to switch. 'It was really no different from what many first-year students go through,' recalled former Palace official Mark Bolland. 'We approached the whole thing as a wobble which was entirely normal.' As William later confessed: 'I

Right: Carley Massy-Birch, with whom William had a close relationship at St Andrews. Her own description of herself as a 'country bumpkin' belied her brains, as well as her beauty.

Left: More from the Prince's 'little black book': Rose Farquhar (left) and Arabella Musgrave, whose father is said to have had a 'quiet word' with William about the couple's public displays of affection.

don't think I was homesick. I was more daunted. My father was very understanding and realized I had the same problem he had had [at Cambridge].'

Once he changed courses he flourished, helped by his first student dalliance with Carley Massy-Birch, the striking brunette whom he had met during his unsuccessful audition for *Franny and Zooey*. Early on in the spring 2002 term he arranged an 'accidental' encounter in the St Salvator's dining room and asked Carley to join him and some friends at a local pub, a familiar tactic to screen her presence in his company. Like other bachelor princes, he ensured that his 'dates' were part of a group so that watchful eyes, clacking tongues and, possibly, long lenses would be frustrated.

Right: William had enjoyed plenty of female company before he went to university. Polo player Natalie Hicks-Löbbecke with the Prince at a polo match in July 2000.

It was a highly successful ruse. Before he went up to St Andrews, William had enjoyed plenty of female company, and kept a well-thumbed little black book of girlfriends and friends who were girls. Yet few had become publicly known, which was precisely as he liked it. In the summer of 2001, for example, he had dated Arabella, the eighteen-year-old daughter of Major Nicholas Musgrave, who managed the Cirencester Park Polo Club. According to at least one report, their public displays of affection obliged the Major to have a quiet word with the ardent Prince. Then there was polo player Natalie 'Nats' Hicks-Löbbecke; farmer's daughter Emma Lippiatt, aged nineteen, who lived near Highgrove; Rose, the daughter of Captain Ian Farquhar, Master of the Beaufort Hunt; and Kate Middleton's erstwhile schoolfellow Emilia d'Erlanger, who had been invited to join William and friends on a summer cruise. Other female friends included Davina Duckworth-Chad, whose brother, James, was an equerry to the Queen; Lady Katherine Howard, daughter of the Earl of Suffolk; Emma Parker Bowles, Camilla's niece; and Alexandra Knatchbull, the great-great-granddaughter of Lord Mountbatten.

All these young women had one quality in common – they were well-bred, discreet and seemingly safe scions of England's squirearchy and aristocracy. Although St Andrews attracted a fair proportion of privately educated upper-class youngsters – what the townsfolk called 'yahs', from their drawled pronunciation of 'yes' – William was now mingling with a wider social and ethnic mix than he had been used to.

For example, it is doubtful whether, under normal social circumstances (normal for royalty, that is), he would ever have set eyes on Carley, the daughter of Devon farmers Mary and Hugh Massy-Birch. While she liked to describe herself as a 'country bumpkin', Carley was not only beautiful but brainy. 'Funny and delightful company', was one verdict on a young woman whose bottom, according to her many admirers, had been 'sculpted by the gods'.

After their relationship became more intimate William was spotted cycling to the house Carley rented in the centre of town. 'Yes, they were lovers,' confirms a close friend. Within a few weeks, however, the novelty of dating the future King wore off, Carley tiring of the endless manœuvring necessary to keep their relationship out of the public eye.

For example, when William paid £200 ($300) for a front-row table at the first ever 'Don't Walk' student charity fashion show, held at the Fairmont St Andrews Hotel on 26 March 2002, Carley was seated at a table near by so that photographers would not be able to snap them together.

It was an evening that changed William's life for ever, albeit not in the way he had imagined. When one of the amateur models, Kate Middleton, sashayed down the catwalk in a sheer shift dress over a bikini, William's reaction was typical: 'She's hot,' he murmured, a phrase he had used before when confronted by the 5-foot-10-inch brunette.

In fact, he was more surprised than almost anyone in the room by the sight of the normally demure Ms Middleton. They had been friends for some months, having met in their first term, when both had been attending lectures for their History of Art course. Indeed, the fact that both had been to Chile during their gap years was an instant point of contact. She would occasionally join him and his friends for breakfast at their table in the St Salvator's dining room, though she was presumably unaware of the male banter about her. Before the fashion show William had felt sufficiently comfortable with her as a friend to ask her to come and live with him and two other students, Olivia Bleasdale and Fergus Boyd, in a house-share for their second year at St Andrews. At that time he saw her as a friend and no more.

If he was taken aback by her appearance, he was not alone. Everyone in her circle was astonished that their rather self-contained friend, whose chief claim to fame was playing college hockey, had the nerve to reveal herself so daringly before such an audience. Fellow student Michael Choong, sitting at an adjacent table, recalls: 'It was hilarious. Kate had already caught his [William's] eye in the Sally dining hall but when he saw the sexy dress he couldn't take his eyes off her. He wasn't the only one. Kate already had a reputation. Everyone knew who she was. She's a very pretty girl and you could hear remarks like: "Oh, yeah! That's fit Kate from Sally's. She's hot."'

The university's Principal, Dr Brian Lang, remembers that evening for rather different reasons. 'One of the male models had stuffed a sock down his underpants. It was very obvious to the audience. I remember myself and one of William's protection officers having a good laugh about it.'

Previous pages: (left) 'When one of the amateur models . . . sashayed down the catwalk in a sheer shift dress over a bikini, William's reaction was typical: "She's hot."' Kate Middleton at the St Andrews students' charity fashion show, March 2002. (right) Kate on the catwalk during the 'Don't Walk' fashion show at St Andrews. It was not this outfit, however, that caught the Prince's – and the world's – attention.

Right: At ease in their own company: the relationship that started and blossomed at university deepened in the years that followed.

WILLIAM
AND KATE

A Street Called Hope

On 30 March 2002, several days after the now historic fashion show, Queen Elizabeth the Queen Mother died, aged 101. If any event defined the difference between William and his fellow students, it was this. From enjoying a carefree night out with his student friends he found himself, only days later, with his brother and father, together with eleven other senior members of the royal family, including the Princess Royal, on live television, walking in the funeral cortége to Westminster Abbey. While the solemn sight inevitably evoked memories of Diana's funeral procession, this time many people's thoughts were with Prince Charles, who was visibly distressed. As Deborah, Duchess of Devonshire wrote of him, 'My poor friend's steely face made us all realize how much he loved her and relied on her.'

While Prince Charles sought consolation in time-honoured fashion by writing letters about his grandmother, his oldest son

followed a more contemporary path, texting and telephoning friends to reflect on his sense of loss and his affection for the woman he and his brother had called 'Gran-Gran'. One of the first people he turned to for consolation was Carley, texting her constantly and calling her at her Devon farm home where she spent the Easter break. Soon afterwards, however, she had moved on, telling the Prince that she was ending their relationship as she was seeing someone else. That was not the only reason. After the initial excitement of dating the heir to the throne, Carley had found the subterfuge wearing. She was smuggled everywhere by his bodyguard to ensure that their romance remained secret. When they were able to spend time alone she found William 'sweet and lovely', but the effort involved in spending private time together was exhausting. Their parting was amicable, however. As with all his exes, William remains on good terms with Carley to this day.

That, shortly afterwards, he began dating one of Carley's friends, a tall and beautiful strawberry blonde, only underscored the observation of several graduates that St Andrews was 'a romantic merry-go-round'. Certainly in his first year at the university Kate Middleton did not appear on his romantic radar. In fact, he was annoyed on her behalf when, days after the fashion

Previous page: Queen Elizabeth the Queen Mother with her great-grandsons on her ninety-ninth birthday, August 1999. The two princes were very fond of the woman they called 'Gran-Gran', who died in March 2002.

Left: The Queen, with Princes William and Edward behind her, next to a visibly upset Prince Charles at the funeral of the Queen Mother, 9 April 2002.

show, a Sunday newspaper headlined the fact that in the coming academic year 'Undie Graduate' Kate was to join William and other students in a rented house. But William was perplexed, too. He began to wonder if someone in his circle was deliberately leaking information, especially as the story appeared as the dust was still settling after revelations in a Sunday tabloid in January about Harry smoking pot.

Whatever his thoughts about Kate, however, at the time she was involved in a romance with an ebullient, curly-haired law student named Rupert Finch. He had a reputation for throwing noisy, champagne-fuelled parties in his flat in St Andrews, some of which William had attended, on at least one occasion making out publicly with Carley's friend. At another party Rupert and Kate sneaked away to his darkened bedroom, only to discover a drunken fellow student sleeping on his bed. As Kate quickly made her exit, Finch cried out 'What the hell is going on?' The unwanted guest later explained, 'I was the wrong guy in the wrong bed at the wrong time.' Shortly afterwards the lights went out on the romance between Kate and Finch when he graduated.

In the summer term, Kate began to move further into William's circle, shyly at first, but as the months went by

Right: Photographs of William and Kate together at St Andrews are rare, partly because of the Palace's agreement with the media that he should be left to complete his education in peace. This shot was taken in the town in April 2003, during their second year at the university.

becoming increasingly comfortable in his company. She herself later admitted, 'It did take a bit of time for us to get to know each other but we did become very close friends from quite early.' Before she left for her summer vacation – during which she worked as a waitress serving drinks at Henley Royal Regatta for £5.25 ($8.50) an hour – she couldn't help but wonder how she would cope with living in the same house as the heir to the throne. Still, whatever happened, it was certainly a story that one day she could tell her grandchildren.

Before they moved in, in September 2002, this royal version of *Friends* had been vetted by Special Branch. Alarms and heavy-duty locks were installed in the four-bedroomed house, and neighbours on Hope Street warned that they would face some disruption to their day-to-day life. As term began police patrols increased, leading other students who lived in the quiet street to joke that it was the second most protected thoroughfare in Britain after Downing Street.

It was all very much above board. Their landlords, the Very Reverend James Whyte, a former Moderator of the General Assembly of the Church of Scotland, and his wife Ishbel lived on the premises, in the basement. It was William who elected himself 'house father', personally writing out and delivering the first cheque to his new landlord before collecting the rent, which was £100 ($160) a week, from the other housemates.

While the discreet – and at times not so discreet – police presence provided other residents with a frisson of excitement, life inside number 13 Hope Street was resolutely domestic. As designated den mother Kate, practical and organized – she was the only one of the foursome who registered on the electoral roll to vote – was keen on making sure the house ran smoothly. As a decent short-order cook (she had learned baking at her mother's knee), she regularly made supper for the quartet.

William was relegated to the trash; it was his job to put out the wheelie bin for collection every week. It took him a while to get the hang of it, often putting the bin out too late. As his landlady Ishbel Whyte noted, 'Why would a lad who lived in a palace place any great importance on putting out the rubbish?' Once Ishbel had trained him he was never late again, and at Kate's prompting he left a generous gratuity for the refuse collectors that Christmas.

During his year-long sojourn as a tenant of the Whytes, William learned other, more profound, lessons. As the head of the Church of Scotland at the time, James Whyte had delivered a moving sermon in memory of the 270 people killed when, on 21 December 1988, a terrorist bomb brought down Pan-Am Flight 103 over Lockerbie in south-west Scotland. William warmed to this wise man of faith and asked if he could profile him and his wife for a college essay. Whyte agreed and the two spent some time discussing his life and times. When Whyte, a learned, witty and charming man, fell ill and had to spend long periods in a Dundee hospital, William ensured that his protection officer was at hand to chauffeur his wife Ishbel to visit him.

Apart from passing the time of day with the Whytes, William would head down to his local supermarket to stock up on supplies, paying with his credit card. He would complain to fellow students about the prices or the odd dietary preferences of his housemates, or would discuss the latest movie he had seen. 'He was determined not to let his status get in the way of his everyday life,' notes a friend. That said, he wasn't above letting fellow students know that he had star pulling power, on one occasion showing off an America's Cup yacht jacket available only to the very few.

There were other glimpses of the bizarre parallel universe William inhabited. One minute he might be putting out the trash, the next, perhaps, in the middle of a raging media storm,

Below: 'He was determined not to let his status get in the way of his everyday life' – William buying magazines in a local newsagent during his second year at university.

Above: Paul Burrell,
former butler to
Diana, Princess
of Wales, outside
the Old Bailey in
London just after
all charges against
him were dropped.
William and Harry
later described
Burrell's memoir of
his time with Diana
as 'a cold and overt
betrayal'.

as in November 2002, just after he had moved into Hope Street. This concerned the collapse of the trial of his mother's butler Paul Burrell, who had been charged with stealing items belonging to the Princess as well as to William and Harry. Trying to balance these two frequently colliding worlds was a continuing test of princely character.

Kate Middleton faced a test of a rather different kind: the dawning realization that William had become, to her, much more than just a housemate. Their shared interest in outdoor pursuits, amateur dramatics and sport – they played tennis together, and she often joined him for rigorous early-morning swimming sessions at a local five-star hotel – as well as their lively senses of humour, provided the springboard for friendship. It was not long before they were diving deeper, friendship flowing seamlessly into romance. Their friends noticed the change almost immediately, although the signs were hardly difficult to spot. In public they never gave a sign of intimacy; in private they couldn't keep their hands off each other. 'They are both frisky people,' observed an intimate with wry understatement.

Kate's behaviour changed, too. Described as 'sweet and unassuming', she became even more reclusive and restrained. If, for example, a girlfriend suggested going out for a drink after

lectures, she was no longer so readily available, 'I've got to meet Will' becoming an almost constant refrain. She treated her prince like a king, too. Invariably the first to wake in the morning, she would prepare breakfast for him – eggs, toast and tea – before he walked to lectures.

While William tried his hand in the kitchen, Kate, as he admitted later, would hover in the background to make sure he didn't cause too much damage. If she didn't cook, the student lovers would spend the evening in front of the TV with an Indian or Chinese takeaway washed down with a few bottles of his favourite Australian lager. If this was no different from thousands of other students, nor were the endless arguments about who was responsible for the washing up. Indeed, it became such a bone of contention that they bought a dishwasher between them.

For William, such mundane domesticity was heaven. He was thoroughly enjoying living in a land called 'normal', as when

Above: Before the wider world knew: Kate snapped with William at rugby practice, St Andrews, March 2003. By now, 'I've got to meet Will' had become her constant refrain when friends asked her out.

he would take his 600cc Yamaha motorcycle for a spin around the winding roads, R&B music playing at full blast. Their neighbour, history student Jules Knight, observed: 'We were all in a safe bubble at St Andrews. Kate and Will could go for a drink and hold hands without anyone noticing.'

Yet inevitably there were constant reminders of William's status. On one occasion he gave a party at the house in Hope Street, only for the fire alarm to go off, causing the Prince to switch off the power supply to silence it. In doing so he also switched off hidden cameras in the house, which in turn alerted the police who arrived at the front door by the vanload. It was a story that would have made headlines, but it remained under wraps until after he had graduated.

Even though the media by and large kept their side of the deal to stay away from St Andrews, William was always wary. At the May Ball in 2003, organized by the men-only Kate Kennedy Club which counted him as a member (Kate was a founder member of a rival all-girl society, the Lumsden Club), the couple were part of a large group so outsiders would never guess that they were dating. However, when Kate watched William play in the rugby sevens that month, and then lay on the grass chatting with him during breaks in play, tongues started wagging. Her father Michael brushed off the gossip. 'We are very amused at the thought of being in-laws to Prince William,' he said. 'But I don't think it is going to happen.'

He may have altered his views somewhat on seeing his daughter's excited reaction when William arrived at the Middletons' home in June 2003 to join in Kate's belated twenty-first-birthday celebrations, which were held in a marquee in the garden. Days later, Kate was one of William's guests when he too celebrated his coming-of-age with a fancy-dress party on the theme of 'Out of Africa', held at Windsor Castle. Everyone, including the Queen, entered into the party

Below: St Andrews nights: Kate as a guest at the all-male Kate Kennedy Club, which organized this first-year jazz night, where she was photographed with a friend, Ed Gribbon.

spirit, Charles Spencer and Prince Andrew dressing as big-game hunters, while William's old flame, Carley Massy-Birch, arrived as a Zulu princess in a costume specially flown over by a South African relative.

The man who stole the show, however, was the self-styled 'comedy terrorist' Aaron Barshak, who literally walked in through a main entrance, unchallenged and uninvited, dressed as the terrorist Osama bin Laden. As Prince William, bare-chested in a Tarzan loincloth, was on stage thanking his father and the Queen for organizing the party, Barshak joined him and grabbed the microphone. It was reported that he even managed to kiss the Prince on both cheeks before being ejected. 'I didn't know my brother could do an accent like that,' William joked when the dust had settled.

He found less to laugh about at the start of his third year at university that autumn. He had decided to move out of Hope Street, instead renting Balgove House, a substantial farmhouse

Right: Between water polo and playing in the rugby sevens, as a student William kept himself pretty fit. Running in a charity race in London in July 2004, during his third year at university.

Left: Jecca, the beautiful daughter of Ian and Jane Craig, William's 'second family' in Kenya. He was often irritated by inaccurate press reports that she was his girlfriend, although she was guest of honour at his twenty-first-birthday party.

set in a large private estate on the outskirts of St Andrews and owned by a friend of the royal family, Henry Cheape. The Prince invited Kate to join him along with two other friends, Alasdair Coutts-Wood and Oli Baker. The auguries were not propitious. On 10 September 2003, shortly before the start of term, Kate's maternal grandfather, Ronald Goldsmith, died of heart failure. The retired builder and lorry driver was only seventy-two. A few weeks later, in October, Diana's former butler, Paul Burrell, published his contentious memoir, *A Royal Duty*, which William and Harry described as a 'cold and overt betrayal'.

Although William was certainly no regular student, he was living far more modestly than had his father at the same age. When Charles was twenty-one he had had an equerry-cum-private secretary, a valet to look after his wardrobe and a driver. William's romance was rather less formal, too. During Charles's courtship of Lady Diana Spencer she had called him 'Sir' until they married. Within the walls of Balgove House Kate called the future King 'Big Willies' while his nickname for her was 'Babykins'.

Once they settled back into a relatively normal routine, Kate discovered that life at Balgove House was on a much grander scale than at her previous digs. William installed an antique polished mahogany table and chairs which seated eighteen, and regularly hosted black-tie dinners. In case someone didn't get the point, presiding over the dining room was a huge, rather battered oil painting of the Queen, and a Union flag. They dined off roast venison from deer that William had shot and which Kate – with a little help – had cooked in the Aga in the kitchen. The wine was decent but not expensive, and when William gave more informal parties they kept the beer cold in the downstairs bath.

Kate, with five other female students including Bryony Daniels, was invited to join the Prince for a pre-Christmas shooting party on the Queen's estate at Sandringham.

For Kate, even given her privileged upbringing, this was a world very different from anything she had been used to. Naturally diffident, she continually deferred to William's judgement, happy to follow in his wake. Her complaisance meant, however, that she was the one who was always compromising. Because William was instinctively wary of outsiders, she mirrored his views, now keeping those of her friends who had never met him at a distance. In time she became more and more reliant on his circle of friends, and as a result neglected her own. Additionally, while their new lodgings gave them more privacy, the place was remote from day-to-day student life, so they were thrown together more than perhaps was desirable at such a young age and so early in their relationship. Obstinate and strong-willed, William could be an overwhelming presence, and at times Kate felt taken for granted, treated like a servant rather than his girlfriend.

That she was the only girl in a testosterone-fuelled environment did not help matters. Michael Choong, who visited the couple at their farmhouse, recalls: 'He could be flip and curt with her. She didn't like it when he ignored her and got into conversation with someone as though she wasn't there. He expected Kate to run after him and the longer they knew each other the more he seemed to keep her on a tight leash. 'There were spats, rows and break-ups as William and Kate tried to find

Right: Michael Choong (left), a friend of both William and Kate at St Andrews, and a shrewd commentator on the Prince's life there, partying with Ed Gribbon and Kate during their university days.

Left: Kate during a skiing trip to Klosters with William and other friends. By now the media – and the public – knew about 'the steady girlfriend'.

their way both as young adults and as a couple. 'It was an edgy relationship,' according to another friend. 'They were always in and out.'

Often their differences boiled down to that age-old divide between men and women: she simply wanted more from him, in terms of emotional commitment and support, than he was prepared to give at that stage of his life. It did not go down well, for example, that when he was in London he visited Purple, the nightclub close to the Chelsea football stadium, and was seen dancing with a variety of young women, none of whom resembled Kate. Yet as turbulent as their romance was and became, she was a steady fixture in his life, a girlfriend who was reliable and true. As she told a friend: 'He's lucky to be going out with me.'

Right: That William attended the wedding of his friend, Ed van Cutsem, to Lady Tamara Grosvenor in November 2004 without Kate led, inevitably, to rumours of a split. From left to right: the Duke of Westminster (the bride's father), William, the Queen, Prince Harry, the Duke of Edinburgh.

It was not until April 2004 that the world had its first real glimpse into William's love life, when Kate joined him and a group of friends on the ski slopes at Klosters in Switzerland. Kate and William were photographed, *The Sun* newspaper publishing the story on its front page under the headline: 'Finally . . . Wills Gets A Girl'. She was well and truly in the media's sights when, in August 2004, he took his Girl Friday with a group of friends to the desert island of Rodrigues, in the Indian Ocean.

Given their proximity during term time, however, it was perhaps sensible that they decided to give each other some space during the long summer vacation. While Kate spent time with her family, William flew to Nashville, Tennessee, to visit an old friend, the American heiress Anna Sloan, and her family on their 360-acre estate.

Shortly afterwards he went on a boys-only yacht cruise around the Greek islands, while Kate joined Fergus Boyd and friends at his family's holiday home in the Dordogne, France.

With so much time spent apart, there were rumours that they had split, based on the 'evidence' that Kate was not present at the wedding of Ed van Cutsem to the Duke of Westminster's daughter, Lady Tamara Grosvenor, in November 2004, a society

occasion attended by both William and Harry as well as the Queen. While the 'were they, weren't they' rumour mill continued to grind during their final year at St Andrews, they were able to spend occasional weekends at Tam-na-Ghar, a cottage on the Balmoral Estate which the Queen had given to William and Harry for their personal use. The lovers were even daring enough to appear as a couple at a college dance during that autumn term. As a further sign that she was William's steady girlfriend, Kate was a guest at Prince Charles's fifty-sixth birthday party, held at Highgrove that same November, and joined all three Waleses on the ski slopes of Klosters a few days before Charles's wedding to Camilla Parker Bowles in April the following year.

It was an eventful few days. As the three princes posed on the slopes for a prearranged photo call, Prince Charles forgot, or perhaps did not know, that his microphone would amplify the comments he whispered to his sons. He referred to the assembled journalists as 'these bloody people', and then went on to disparage the BBC's royal correspondent, Nicholas Witchell, saying, 'I can't bear that man. I mean, he's so awful, he really is.'

Kate, however, was more concerned about some unguarded remarks that William made to a journalist at the local Casa Antica nightclub during an aprés-ski evening when his extrovert friend Guy Pelly jumped into the lap of *The Sun's* royal reporter wearing nothing but a pair of gold silk boxer shorts. In answer to a question about his own marriage, the Prince replied: 'Look, I'm only twenty-two, for God's sake. I am too young to marry at my age. I don't want to get married until I'm at least twenty-eight

Above: June 2005, and the end of university beckons. Kate photographed with her father, Michael Middleton, in St Andrews on the day that she and William graduated.

or maybe thirty.' While this may have been a little too blunt and matter-of-fact for Kate's liking, at least she now knew how the land lay. If she wanted to stand by the man she loved, she would be standing for several years to come.

Moreover, she knew that, post-university, William was headed for a military career, which in any case would take him away from her for long periods. Yet if she was perturbed, she didn't show it, seemingly unruffled and all smiles even as she was surrounded by a scrum of photographers, when in June, shortly after her Finals, she attended the Oxfordshire wedding of Hugh van Cutsem and Rose Astor, at which once again William was an usher. It was the first society event at which they had appeared together, William having attended his father's marriage in Windsor two months earlier on his own. Shortly afterwards they were photographed together again, licking one another's ice cream cones at a polo tournament at the Beaufort Club near the Highgrove estate, where Kate had been among the guests celebrating William's twenty-third birthday.

Then they headed north to St Andrews, graduating with the rest of their class at a formal ceremony on 23 June 2005, an event marked by the attendance not only of Prince Charles and his new bride, now known by the title Duchess of Cornwall, but also the Queen and Duke of Edinburgh. They looked on as William, in a black gown, tail coat and white tie, was called to the stage to receive an upper second-class degree in Geography, while Kate graduated with the same class of degree in History of Art.

On the night after William graduated, university officials, officers from the local police force and from Special Branch, Palace advisers and others who had been responsible for ensuring the Prince's safety and well-being during his time at St Andrews, met for a celebratory party in a town-centre pub. Such a celebration at the end of a royal tour abroad is known as 'wheels-up', for it is held once a royal has flown out of the country. This quiet affair was called a 'Wills-up', as everyone breathed a collective sigh of relief at a job well done.

The Principal of St Andrews, Dr Brian Lang, sagely, and perhaps presciently, reflected, 'We enabled Prince William to have the four most normal years of his life – a period of normality that he had never had before and will never have again.'

Right: HRH Prince William of Wales, MA (Geography); his father is beside him. This photograph was taken just after he had graduated.

Left: Miss Catherine Middleton, MA (History of Art), University of St Andrews.

WILLIAM AND KATE

The End of the Affair?

When Diana, Princess of Wales, talked on the telephone – which was often – midway through a conversation she would suddenly say, 'Hello boys, time to change the tape.' It was a joke with an uncharacteristically bitter twist. The Princess believed not only that the Palace was conspiring against her, but that the security forces were routinely tapping her telephones.

With hindsight, it is easy to understand why. For years she had been dismissed as 'deranged and paranoid' for suspecting that her husband was involved in a clandestine relationship with his married friend – and former flame – Camilla Parker Bowles. As the world now knows, there was in fact an elaborate conspiracy to keep that relationship secret. The strain of the day-to-day subterfuge actually made some of his staff physically ill.

For Diana, there was no joy in this discovery, made public in January 1993, when a British tabloid published an illicit recording of a telephone call between Charles and Camilla. Just months earlier, Diana's own conversation with her lover, James Gilbey – the now notorious 'Squidgygate' tapes – had also hit the headlines.

So it was hardly surprising that the covert activities of the secret services, real or perceived, were often discussed by Diana. Far from being a symptom of paranoia, they had proved to be simply a fact of her dislocated life. After the profound shock of her untimely death in August 1997 a healthy minority of the public, including Dodi Fayed's grieving father, Mohammed, believed that Diana and her boyfriend had been the victims of an elaborate assassination plot.

As young adults, Diana's sons were gaining a fresh appreciation of what their mother had gone through. During the spring and summer of 2005 it seemed that nothing they said or did, from Harry's visit to a lap-dancing club with fellow Army officers to William's birthday gift for his father, remained private.

Every time they went out in public, a photographer would appear, as if from nowhere. It was unnerving and deeply irritating. They simply could not trust a soul.

At university, William had faced a similar problem of trust. He laid false trails, making up stories which he fed to those he suspected of treachery. The chief suspect, a female student, was ostracized by the Prince and his circle. As his student friend Michael Choong observed: 'Will didn't suffer fools gladly and he detested people who sneaked on him to the media. He's certainly not a vindictive guy but you can forget it if you abuse his trust.'

As it had for their mother, normal life – or what passes for normal life inside the royal family – was becoming intolerable. There seemed to be no dividing line between what was personal and what was public. More than that, it seemed to William and Harry that there were numerous so-called 'friends' inside their different circles who were tipping off the media about their movements. For a young man who liked to be in control of his life, William felt constantly beleaguered.

Below: Late in 2005, *The News of the World* published a piece which said that William had injured his knee during a kickabout – seen here – with youngsters at the Charlton Athletic ground in south-east London. This, with other details reported in the paper that were known only to a handful of the Prince's intimates, convinced him that someone was leaking information about him.

This feeling inevitably communicated itself to his girlfriend, leaving Kate terrified to tell anyone anything about her life. It was all-consuming. As one intimate of the Prince told me: 'For years [William and Harry] had been living with suspicion about their friends and colleagues, not knowing who was briefing. They thought that the world was against them, believed that they were being betrayed by all and sundry as every week there was something that could only have come from someone inside the royal camp. As a result they distrusted everyone.'

Of course, blaming others was sometimes a way of avoiding responsibility, as when, early in 2005, Prince Harry hired an Afrika Korps costume, complete with swastika armband, for a friend's fancy-dress party. A fellow guest simply used his camera phone to snap the prince, and sold the image and the story to the tabloids. Such juvenile lapses in taste and judgement notwithstanding, it was the drip, drip, drip of minor but intimate details that was wearing.

With a delicious irony that would have amused their late mother, her own experience finally unlocked the riddle. Diana's ghost was about to take revenge on her tabloid tormentors.

In November 2005 William met a friend, ITV political correspondent Tom Bradby, at Clarence House. A previously scheduled meeting, to discuss William's borrowing equipment

to edit videos from his gap year and student days, had been cancelled at short notice. Curiously, however, a sarcastic diary item in the previous Sunday's *News of the World* by veteran royal correspondent Clive Goodman had confidently stated that William had *already* borrowed the equipment. Only three people, Bradby, William and his new private secretary, Jamie Lowther-Pinkerton, had known about the meeting.

Moreover, the week before, Goodman had revealed how William was undergoing physiotherapy for a knee injury he had sustained during a kickabout with youngsters at a football ground, as a result of which he had had to pull out of a mountain-rescue course. Again, fewer than a handful of trusted people had known that William was seeing a knee surgeon.

When they met in his office, Prince William made it clear that he did not suspect Bradby, a sometime thriller writer, of any leaks. Instead, as they reflected upon the uncannily accurate stories, Bradby remembered a conversation some years previously with the paparazzo who had taken a telling picture of Diana getting out of a car owned by the *Daily Mail*'s royal correspondent, Richard Kay. Since Kay had effectively been her mouthpiece for several years, the picture had confirmed widespread rumours of collusion between the Princess and the reporter.

Left: Diana, Princess of Wales with the *Daily Mail*'s royal correspondent, Richard Kay. It was from knowledge that Kay's mobile phone had been hacked for details about his secret meetings with Diana that William and others were able to discover how *The News of the World* was obtaining highly confidential information about the two princes.

Right: Clive Goodman, *The News of the World*'s royal correspondent until the phone-hacking scandal broke, arrives at Westminster Magistrates' Court in August 2006. He and a private detective on the paper's payroll, Glen Mulcaire, were both sent to prison for illegally hacking telephones, those of William's aides among them.

William listened intently as Bradby told a story that might have come from one of his thrillers. Knowing that on most mornings Diana sent a voicemail or text to Kay's mobile phone, photographers would hack into his phone before he opened his messages. The technique was simple: after ensuring that Kay's mobile was switched off, they waited for the recording asking the caller to leave a message, then punched in the code programmed as a security number – 4444, say, or a similar repetition of a digit – which gave them instant access to messages.

William and his private secretary were thunderstruck. 'If this potentially is happening to us, then who on earth else could this be happening to?' observed Lowther-Pinkerton, whose military service with the SAS had left him no stranger to the dark arts. The fact that Goodman seemed to know what was going on in the royal family down to the tiniest detail – even the fact that William was having a photograph of Prince Charles's favourite foxhound framed for his birthday – suggested that he and perhaps others were behind this illegal practice.

Lowther-Pinkerton called in the head of the Royalty Protection Branch, who passed the inquiry to Scotland Yard's Counter-Terrorism Command. During the course of the six-month investigation they discovered that other members of the Royal Household had been targeted, as had a number of public figures and celebrities, including, allegedly, supermodel Elle

Left: William and Harry in 2005 – by then both princes had become extremely suspicious about leaks to the media concerning their activities.

Macpherson, Liberal Democrat MP Simon Hughes and Gordon Taylor, the chairman of the Professional Footballers' Association. Goodman and a private detective, Glen Mulcaire, who had been on the payroll of the *News of the World*, received prison sentences for illegally intercepting telephone messages.

The fall-out continues to this day, for few believe that the practice was the work of a lone 'rogue reporter', as News International, owners of the *News of the World,* have argued. Shortly after the trial, Andy Coulson, the newspaper's editor, resigned, going on to work as head of communications for David Cameron, then Leader of the Opposition and now the Prime Minister. In January 2011 Coulson resigned from that post after the publication of new revelations and concerns about phone-tapping inside British newspapers.

Both William and Harry felt a profound and enduring sense of relief, albeit tinged with guilt about suspecting innocent people. 'The phone-tapping scandal was a transformative moment for [the princes] in their dealings with the outside world,' a friend observed. 'From then on they were able to relax. They were able to have a private circle who wouldn't betray them, nor did they have to put them to any test. At last they were able to distinguish between their private and public lives.'

As for Kate Middleton, she appreciated how Diana must have felt. Kate had endured her own doubts, terrified to tell anyone anything about her life and wondering whether William might suspect someone close to her. While discretion had been the watchword in St Andrews, this was new territory for her, the carefree intimacy of university life gone for ever.

Upon graduation, the real world muscled into their lives. In less time than it took to say 'Big Willies', Kate's boyfriend was transformed into Prince William of Wales, metaphorically enrolling in an intensive, tailor-made post-graduate course that was, as it were, fit for a prince. In June 2005, William flew to New Zealand on his first overseas visit as the Queen's representative to commemorate the sixtieth anniversary of the end of the Second World War. During the brief trip he managed to rub shoulders with the British Lions rugby team, only to see them crash to defeat against the New Zealand All Blacks. Then it was on to Kenya, spending August learning about conservation on the magnificent Lewa Downs estate owned by his friends and 'second family', Ian and Jane Craig, who run a sanctuary for black rhinos and other endangered animals. The arrival of Kate and some friends for a week-long holiday, the first time the couple had been together since their graduation, finally dispelled the gossip about William and Jecca Craig.

At the end of August they managed a night out at Purple, the Chelsea nightclub, Kate sitting on her boyfriend's knee, possibly wishing to keep him in one place for a time. It was a forlorn hope. In September William joined the Queen at Balmoral, before taking on his first internship, learning about land management at Chatsworth, the grand 35,000-acre country seat of the Duke and Duchess of Devonshire in the Peak District. He even donned an apron and worked in the butcher's shop. 'A wonderful place to stay but don't try to tackle the stairs once you have a drink!' 'Will from Gloucestershire' wrote in the ducal visitors' book, before changing into a pinstriped suit and setting out for the City of London, where he shadowed bankers at HSBC, then briefly visited the Bank of England, the London Stock Exchange and other financial institutions. In December the pinstripe became a flying suit as he spent a couple of weeks with the mountain rescue team from RAF Valley in Anglesey, North Wales. During training – the course delayed because of his now infamous knee

Below: With the RAF Valley mountain-rescue team in Wales, December 2005. His experiences probably contributed to his later decision to become a search-and-rescue helicopter pilot.

injury – he abseiled down a 200-foot cliff with a stretcher dangling beneath him. Meanwhile, he had passed the Army's Regular Commissions Board selection process and been accepted for a forty-four-week course in officer training at the Royal Military Academy, Sandhurst, which was due to start in January 2006. 'I am only too well aware, having spoken so much to Harry, this is just the beginning,' he said. 'I am really looking forward to taking my place alongside all the other cadets at Sandhurst.'

Below: Major-General Ritchie, Commandant of the RMA, Sandhurst, greets Prince William and his father on the former's arrival to start the officer-training course at the academy. General Ritchie made it clear that the Prince would receive no different treatment from the other officer-cadets.

Before reporting for duty, he took his girlfriend for a short skiing holiday in Klosters, where the normally cautious Prince was pictured stealing a kiss from Kate. Or rather, from 'my adorable Kate', as he referred to her at the surprise farewell party for him that she organized at Clarence House. Then Officer Cadet Wales left for five weeks' basic training, out of contact with family and friends. During gruelling days that began at dawn and ended late into the night, he learnt the intricacies of drill, weapon handling and making his bed the Sandhurst way. 'I can assure you that he will be treated the same as every other cadet,' said Major-General Andrew Ritchie. 'They need to know what it is like to be tired and to be hungry, to lead their soldiers in demanding situations around the world.'

As she waited for her prince to come home, Kate realized that she had signed up for a life of long goodbyes, endless texting and haphazard phone calls. All she could do, as a military wife-in-waiting, was adopt the wartime slogan 'Keep calm and carry

Left: Sport remained an important part of William's life. He is seen here trying to ride off his brother during a polo match.

on.' Like other royal girlfriends before her, she was left to fend for herself, aware that she was being constantly judged. Any foolish or thoughtless move, even a word out of place, might easily torpedo her romance.

The only practical advice from Clarence House had come via Paddy Harverson, Prince Charles's communications director, who told her to hold her head up and smile in public. Yet even such innocent gestures were fraught with traps: smile too broadly and it would look as though she was enjoying the limelight. Smile too little, and courtiers might conclude that she couldn't stand the pressure. Even so, she demonstrated that she could take the heat at a horse show at Princess Anne's estate in August 2005, coolly telling the paparazzi, 'If I pose for photos now, you'll want me to pose at other events.' As one royal watcher, Judy Wade, observed, 'It seems she expects to be in the royal fold for a long time.'

In public all she could do was behave like a swan on a stream: appearing calm and serene on the surface, but paddling like hell underwater. Diana would have sympathized completely; even as her engaging smile, winsome manner and impeccable behaviour had endeared her to the public, she had known she was walking a tightrope. As Diana's former flatmate Carolyn Bartholomew recalled: 'She played it just right. She didn't in any way splash it across the newspapers because that ruined her sister's chances. [Sarah Spencer, a former girlfriend of Prince Charles, had given a newspaper interview during her courtship.] Diana was very aware that if anything special had to be cultivated it should take place without any pressure from the press.' The constant stress tested Diana to the limit, however. 'I cried like a baby to the four walls,' she later told me. 'I just couldn't cope with it.'

Yet Lady Diana Spencer had a title, lived in a stately home and knew the royal family as neighbours. Kate had none of those social advantages. While she was slaving in the kitchen, he might be chatting with the titled son or daughter of some rich and aristocratic family. The insecurities inherent in a budding romance are felt all the more keenly when a commoner falls in love with prince.

Kate would, too, have sensed the reservations about her in certain quarters. While she was seen as a 'pretty and sensible' girl, there were those in royal and aristocratic (or would-be aristocratic) circles – it is hard to know how many – who believed

Left: The couple at the Eton Field Game, in which William played, in March 2006; by now they were at ease enough not to worry about being photographed kissing in public.

Right: Kate would have been aware of the – largely snobbish – reservations about her in some quarters. In public, however, she looked as composed as ever.

that the Middletons were, well, too middle-of-the-road for the House of Windsor. 'It was felt that she wasn't from the right stock,' said one Scottish nobleman, speaking on condition of anonymity. 'William was expected to find a suitable bride among the aristocracy or European royalty. One of his own kind. Kate was treated abominably behind her back by some who should have shown better manners.'

If an undercurrent of snobbery and doubt remained, on the surface Kate was welcomed into the fold. When she arrived, unescorted, at the Cheltenham races in March 2006, Prince Charles and Camilla invited her to join them in the royal box for lunch. Press reports described her demeanour with the royal family as 'comfortable'. Certainly she was now confident enough to kiss William in public when she went to watch him play in the Eton Field Game on the following day.

Far too comfortable for some, it seemed, as she flitted from high-society wedding to glamorous red-rope event to exotic holiday, whether Mustique in the Caribbean in May, or yachting around Ibiza in August, albeit with her prince in tow.

While Kate was enjoying the late-night London club scene, courtesy of the Bank of Mum and Dad, her boyfriend often spent his nights sleeping rough on the Welsh bracken, or under a hedgerow in Cyprus during an exhausting military exercise. After more than a year without any visible employment, apart from a somewhat unconvincing story that she had attempted to launch a children's clothing line, she earned the unwanted title 'Waity Katie'. It seemed that, rather than attempt to break through the glass ceiling in commerce, Kate was happy to wait for her prince to slip the glass slipper on her foot – hardly a role model for an ambitious generation of independent young women. In a tart profile of the potential future queen, writer Camilla Long imagined the scene at Kate's home in Bucklebury: 'Inside Kate waits, surfing the web or shuffling snaps, changing occasionally for tennis or tea.' Ironically, it was her family and her home, where William quietly spent time on weekend army leave, that were ultimately to prove her secret weapon.

As Kate became more of a fixture in William's life – a photo of them looking lovingly at one another as they left the London nightclub Boujis in September 2006 reinforced the belief that they were destined to marry – her family began to take

Below: Kate and Pippa Middleton at Cheltenham Races in March 2006. By now, both sisters were occasionally subject to the sort of snobbery that a small section of British Society delights in.

Above: Kate with her parents at the Sovereign's Parade at Sandhurst, when William 'passed out' of the academy as an officer, August 2006. With weary inevitability, Carole Middleton was criticized for, among other things, chewing gum in front of the Queen during the ceremony (she was trying to stop smoking).

centre stage. With her younger sister Pippa now at Edinburgh University and dating 'turbocharged toffs' – young men with titles and money – the girls were dubbed the 'Wisteria sisters' in that they were, according to *Tatler* magazine, 'highly decorative, terribly fragrant and have a ferocious ability to climb.' These unwelcome nicknames – Wisteria Sisters and Waity Katie – perfectly encapsulated a peculiarly British characteristic, a toxic combination of puritanism and snobbery, tinged, perhaps, with envy.

This same quality was on display in December 2006, when Kate and her parents were invited to watch Prince William's passing-out parade at Sandhurst. As the cadets marched smartly past the Queen, the Duke of Edinburgh, Prince Charles and the Duchess of Cornwall, Carole Middleton, sitting with her husband and daughter in the front row, was seen to be chewing gum. Although the nicotine gum was to help her stop smoking, she was criticized for showing disrespect to the ceremony and to her sovereign. When it later emerged that she used 'non-U' (that is, not upper-class) English, for instance referring to the lavatory as a 'toilet', and that William's upper-class friends thought it amusing to shout 'Doors to manual!' when speaking of the former airline stewardess – a story denied by Clarence House – it reinforced some commentators' view that Kate did not have the 'breeding' to become Queen.

But such insinuations failed to spoil William's big day. 'I love the uniform. So, so sexy,' a lip reader hired by a TV station spotted Kate telling her mother, as Officer-Cadet Wales marched past, wearing a red sash to identify him as an escort of the Sovereign's Banner. Like his brother, he opted to join the Blues and Royals (Royal Horse Guards and 1st Dragoons), a regiment of the Household Cavalry.

It was a big day for Kate, too, the first time she had appeared at an official royal engagement, and she made a distinctive debut in a broad-brimmed black hat, black boots and a vibrant red coat. The comparisons with the late Diana, Princess of Wales, who had once worn a similar outfit, were inevitable, and would continue for the foreseeable future, even as Kate began to become a style icon in her own right.

Yet what was arguably the moment of her greatest triumph sowed the seeds for the breakdown of her five-year romance with William. Her arrival at Sandhurst signalled the seriousness of her

Below: Prince William and other officer-cadets march past the saluting base during the Sovereign's Parade. As right marker, William does not 'eyes right' as the squad draws level with the Queen taking the salute.

Above: On her birthday in January 2007, Kate was all but overwhelmed by paparazzi, following intense speculation that her engagement to William was about to be announced. Distressed, she consulted the royal family's lawyers to put an end to the harassment.

royal relationship, so much so that Woolworths started work on wedding souvenirs. Speculation about an engagement reached a crescendo on her twenty-fifth birthday in January 2007. She was now working as an assistant buyer for Jigsaw, a women's-clothing chain owned by Belle and John Robinson, who had recently lent Kate and William their villa on Mustique. Most mornings Kate ran the gauntlet of paparazzi, keeping her head high and smiling, seemingly unconcerned by the fuss. On her birthday, however, mayhem broke out, with dozens of cameramen jostling one another to get their shots. For once, the young woman expected to be the next princess was overwhelmed.

The incident brought echoes of Diana's struggles with the media. Infuriated as well as unnerved, Kate consulted the royal family's lawyers, Harbottle & Lewis, while William issued his own statement: 'Prince William is very unhappy at the paparazzi harassment of his girlfriend. He wants more than anything for it to stop. Miss Middleton should, like any other private individual, be able to go about her everyday business without this kind of intrusion. The situation is proving unbearable for all concerned.'

Days later, the *News of the World*'s royal editor, Clive Goodman, was sentenced to four months in prison for his role in the phone-tapping scandal. But if the royals had decisively won this skirmish, it certainly hadn't ended the conflict with a 24/7 media. In the never-ending war between press and Palace, what happened to Kate Middleton was collateral damage. The longer William hesitated about marrying her, the longer she would remain at the mercy of intrusive journalists. In short, the answer to her problems lay with William. It was time for him to make up his mind.

The idea that the paparazzi and the tabloid media, which he loathed, could influence the most important decision in his life only made him dig in his heels. That, at least, was his rationalization. There was also an emotional conflict: while Kate had made it clear that she wanted a commitment from her man, Prince William, according to close friends, was not so sure.

Siren voices were calling, suggesting that the grass was greener on the other side of the fence. Of course, for a prince of the realm the grass is always greener. The Victorian constitutionalist Walter Bagehot elegantly described the enticements facing a red-blooded royal: 'All the world and the glory of it, whatever is most attractive, whatever is most seductive, has always been offered to the Prince of Wales of the day, and always will be. It is not rational to expect the best virtue where temptation is applied in the most trying form at the frailest time of human life.'

For an unsettled suitor, temptation came in the form of his fellow officers of the Blues and Royals, nicknamed the 'Booze and Royals'. William found himself juggling his romance with night-time drinking sessions with his new Army friends. Not that he was unduly neglecting Kate: in February he took her out to their favourite London clubs and in March on a skiing break with friends to Zermatt, in between low-key visits to her family home.

Below: In fact, press attention had been building for some time, as this picture of the couple, taken as they left a London nightclub in September 2006, shows.

Right: William and Kate on holiday in Ibiza, September 2006 – never far from intrusive journalists and photographers.

Nevertheless, the fault lines in their romance were exposed in late March, when he went to Dorset for a tank-commander's course with other Blues and Royals officers. He was photographed, clearly the worse for drink, in a nightclub with one arm round a blonde and the other around a Brazilian brunette, his hand over her breast.

The juxtaposition of the Prince acting like a bachelor having a good time and the last picture of him and Kate together, wearing dowdy matching tweed outfits at the Cheltenham races in March while looking gloomy and ill at ease, indicated that all was not well in Wills's World.

In April, much to Kate's distress, William ended their relationship. It was a storm that had been brewing a long time, arising from his unwillingness to commit and the feeling his friends noted that 'he could do better'. Whether or not he liked to admit it, the raucous behaviour of the paparazzi on Kate's birthday had forced him to make up his mind.

On 13 April, the night before *The Sun* broke the story of the split, William was with friends at Mahiki, a nightclub in Piccadilly. Studiously avoiding the gazes of circling females, he danced to a Rolling Stones standard, 'You Can't Always Get What You Want'. In the first flush of relief that accompanies the ending of a relationship, he may have thought the refrain was a rebuke to his former lover. It would not be long, though, before the lyrics applied to his own love life.

Right: By March 2007 it was clear that all was not well between William and Kate, as this picture, taken at Cheltenham Races, indicates. Not long afterwards, in April, William ended their relationship.

WILLIAM –
AND CATHERINE

'A Total Shock . . .'

*I*n April 2007, when Clarence House unofficially let the world know that the romance between William and Kate had run its course, few of her friends shed a tear. The prevailing reaction of most of them was, 'Thank goodness that's over.'

For years they had watched helplessly as Kate, whose university dissertation had been on Lewis Carroll, had gradually disappeared down the royal rabbit hole into the Windsor wonderland, leaving her friends out in the cold. 'During her time with William she upset a lot of friends by not making the effort to see them,' noted one of her circle.

As she mourned a failed relationship, she turned back to her family and friends. In mid-April, just days before the break-up was announced in that unofficial court circular, *The Sun*, she joined her mother in Dublin to support their friend, the landscape artist Gemma Billington, at her first solo show. Demure in a polka-dot dress, Kate smiled for the camera but kept her own counsel.

She maintained a similar silence in the days that followed. All her friends offered the same advice: keep smiling, keep busy, just carry on. Even the Prime Minister, Tony Blair, argued that the couple should be allowed to 'get on with their lives'.

Away from the maddening crowd, Kate sought solitude in the country, going for long hacks on the horse she kept stabled near her parents' home. Still, she heeded the advice of family and friends that, socially, she had to get back on her horse. Invariably supported by her sister Pippa, she sipped cocktails – including one appropriately named Good-Time Girl – and danced the night away at Mahiki and Boujis with friends from William's circle, as well as new admirers. Demonstrating that the party must go on, she also attended a high-society book launch at Asprey, the up-market London jewellers, and the VIP stand at the Badminton Horse Trials, before flying off for a weekend break in Ibiza with a group of friends.

It seemed as if she didn't have a care in the world – which was exactly the impression the young woman now voted by the snobs' bible, *Tatler* magazine, as the 'most wanted' party guest, sought to give. In the time-honoured tactic of discarded lovers, pictures of Kate laughing and having fun could only remind the Prince of what he was missing.

To reinforce her carefree, independent new image, she asked one of her oldest friends, Alicia Fox-Pitt, if she could join an all-female group called The Sisterhood who planned to paddle a Chinese dragon boat twenty-one miles across the English Channel to raise money for charity. The Sisterhood – which included a professional ballerina, a model, a woman who had rowed the Atlantic single-handed, and a couple of ultra-marathon runners – billed themselves as 'an elite group of female athletes, talented in many ways, toned to perfection, with killer looks, on a mission to keep boldly going where no girl has gone before.' Kate was entering a world where women did not wait on their men.

Alicia warned her about the gruelling training – at least three dawn sessions a week – and the fact that the exotic entrepreneurial activities of the event's organizer, Emma Sayle, might attract unwelcome publicity. Under the banner 'Killing Kittens', Emma, a diplomat's daughter, arranged sophisticated sex parties which enabled women to explore their sexual fantasies in a safe environment. Kate was undaunted. After all, during her estrangement, the relentlessly well-behaved Ms Middleton had

Above: Much in demand: Kate at the launch party for Simon Sebag-Montefiore's *Young Stalin*, held at Asprey, jewellers by appointment to the Prince of Wales, in May 2007.

kicked back a little, wearing bunny ears at a party held to promote a documentary about the Rampant Rabbit 'adult toy'.

In late April she arrived bright and early for her first 6.30-a.m. training session on the River Thames. Recognizing that Kate was an experienced sailor, the Sisterhood's coach, Cameron Taylor, quickly promoted her to helmswoman, charged with steering the boat across the world's busiest shipping lane. Although Emma Sayle's racy business soon caught the notice of the tabloids, Kate appeared unfazed, even when paparazzi began appearing at their West London training sessions.

It was not too many weeks later that her teammates noticed her on her mobile phone after training, clearly talking to 'you know who', her conversations increasingly peppered with references to 'Wills'. Her strategy seemed to be working.

In between the billing and cooing, their phone calls doubtless touched now and then on his own somewhat larger-scale charity commitments. Since December, William and Harry had overseen the planning for the Concert for Diana, a televised event that was to take place at Wembley Stadium on 1 July 2007 – what would have been Diana's forty-sixth birthday. The twenty-three acts included Diana's favourite band, Duran Duran, and Elton John, who had memorably sung at her funeral almost ten years earlier. Fondly remembering their mother dancing barefoot to Michael

Below: Steering a steady course: at the helm of the dragon boat during training on the River Thames in London for 'The Sisterhood Challenge'.

Left: William and Harry at Wembley Stadium on the day before the Concert for Diana, to mark the tenth anniversary of their mother's death. Kate was at the concert – and at Clarence House afterwards.

Jackson in her sitting room, the princes wanted to convey her love of life, sense of fun, and passion for dance and musicals.

During an interview with US *Today* show host Matt Lauer at Clarence House in April, just after his break-up with Kate, William was upbeat and amusing, constantly sparring with his younger brother about their relative intelligence, their nicknames – 'Ginger' for Harry, 'Wombat' for William – and their ambitions. When asked what Harry would do if he wasn't a royal, his brother interjected, 'Play computer games and drink beer.' Certainly William displayed little sign of suffering a romantic hangover.

The night before the concert, however, Harry had the last laugh. While they were watching singer Joss Stone, a favourite of William's, rehearse, he was asked whether Kate had been invited to the show. For once, the normally fluent Prince was lost for words, stumbling and stuttering over a very non-committal response.

Laughing, Harry said, 'Really well avoided, William, very diplomatic.' Of course Harry knew exactly what was going on backstage in his brother's love life. William's faltering answer concealed the fact that Kate would be spending that night with him at Clarence House.

At the concert Kate sat a row behind William and Harry, frequently glancing in the direction of her prince. Even to the TV audience the rapprochement was obvious, not least when Kate sang every word of the Take That song 'Back For Good'. At the after-party the couple danced in each other's arms, oblivious to the stares of other guests.

In fact, they had kept their reconciliation secret for several weeks. The couple had met, for the first time since the break-up, at Clarence House in late May, and in June Kate had attended a fancy-dress party at William's Army camp at Bovington, the couple kissing on the dance floor. For William, it seemed, the romantic grass was not so green on the other side after all. At heart he was the kind of old-fashioned man who is attracted to home, hearth and family. The very normality of life with Kate, as well as the steadiness of her family – he eventually began calling Michael Middleton 'Dad' – had a profound appeal for a young man who, when all was said and done, was the product of an unhappy marriage within an often distant, and occasionally chilly, family.

As one of his close friends told me: 'He thought he could do better, but realized very quickly what he had given up. William saw pictures of Kate coming out of Boujis or wherever looking stunning and without a care in the world. Quite frankly, he didn't like the idea of another guy enjoying a roll in the hay with his girl. They had had an up-and-down relationship at St Andrews because of his refusal to commit. After the break-up he realized what he really wanted in life. A kid from a broken home finds love, affection and warmth in a stable, steady family.' In effect, Carole and Michael Middleton were the ace with which Kate trumped a future king. As family friend Gemma Billington observed, 'The Middletons are a very close family who have meals together, watch movies, play sports and go on holidays together.' Just what William wanted. His split from Kate had lasted just five weeks.

There was, however, one casualty of this romantic reunion: Kate herself. Or so some of her girlfriends believed, feeling that she was giving up independence for conformity, adventure for safety. When she pulled out of the dragon-boat race in August with just a week to go, their worst fears were confirmed.

In the weeks leading up to the race she and the rest of the crew had posed for pictures for *Hello!* magazine to help publicize their charity efforts. The magazine chose to focus only on Kate, implying that she had given them exclusive access, which was not the case. Since the lawyers acting for her, Harbottle & Lewis, had already threatened media outlets about intrusions into her privacy, her appearance on the magazine cover seemed to undercut the argument that she should be treated as an ordinary person.

Ironically, however, the renewal of her royal romance meant that she was now

Below: The more William saw pictures in the press of Kate having a good time without him, the more he realized what he was missing. She is seen here leaving London nightclub Boujis in mid-May 2007.

Below: Emma Sayle (standing), organizer of the cross-Channel dragon-boat race, with Kate and the Sisterhood crew as they practise on the Thames.

seen as a future queen-in-waiting, without the same 'reasonable expectation of privacy' as the average young woman. Even so, her lawyers advised her to withdraw from the race for which she had trained so hard, in order to safeguard her status as a 'private citizen'.

In an emotional phone call, organizer Emma Sayle told her: 'Remember, this is not just for charity, it is for yourself. Please don't drop out. For the first time in your life you are actually doing something for yourself.' In vain: at a pivotal moment in her life, Kate chose to play by the rules, following the advice of the royal family's legal counsel.

Her friend Alicia Fox-Pitt also had to drop out after breaking her collar bone in a riding accident. Alicia, however, travelled to Dover to wave the team off on what proved to be a world-record-breaking endeavour. As for Kate, it was as if the last three months of relative independence had become another country. The Sisterhood never heard from her again; not so much as a word of congratulation or a donation to the children's charities for which the women raised more than £100,000 ($160,000). As Emma Sayle recalls: 'It was one of the worst experiences of my life. I rue the day I ever met Kate Middleton. She is a lovely girl, but everything that comes with her – the paparazzi, the egos, and Clarence House – make it a nightmare.'

While Emma was helming the dragon boat across the choppy Channel, Kate and William, under the assumed names of Martin and Rose Middleton, were bidding farewell to the paradise island of Desroches in the Outer Seychelles, where they had spent a sublime week renewing their love affair. William returned in time for the service, held at the Guards Chapel, London, at

147

the end of August, to commemorate the tenth anniversary of his mother's death.

The long-delayed inquest into Diana's death began a few weeks later, yet it seemed that the paparazzi had learned nothing from the tragedy. In October, when Kate and William emerged from Boujis in the early hours of the morning, all hell broke loose, the couple aggressively pursued by photographers. The Prince, who told friends afterwards that he found this behaviour 'incomprehensible', seriously considered taking legal action.

Not all photographers were beyond the pale, however. A select group was allowed past the red rope in November when Kate curated her first ever photographic exhibition, arranging the work of celebrity photographer Alistair Morrison at a trendy London gallery. 'She has a good eye,' noted Morrison, a quality that clearly came through in her personal style.

The uninvited long lens remained on the couple's trail, however, when they joined Charles and Camilla for a weekend at Balmoral that winter, where Kate was pictured wearing camouflage gear to stalk stags on the 40,000-acre estate. At Windsor Great Park she was photographed helping carry the birds during a pheasant shoot. Yet when the couple, wearing hats in a vain attempt at disguise, went skating at Somerset House in London, it was an amateur photographer who snapped them.

With the bookies no longer taking bets on the couple marrying, it seemed that all the Prince had to do to end the endless speculation – and paparazzi intrusion – was to make a decent woman of the girl waiting to say: 'I will.' William, who laughs off suggestions that he is stubborn, had other ideas. His personal life had to come second to his career. This now involved a four-month attachment, beginning in January 2008, to the RAF College at Cranwell in Lincolnshire. After weeks of intensive flying training he had earned his wings and, at a ceremony at Cranwell on 11 April, Kate looked on proudly as the coveted flying badge was pinned to the tunic of Flying Officer William Wales by the visiting Air Chief Marshal – who just happened to be his father.

With the graduation ceremony over, William, the fourth generation of the royal family to qualify as an RAF pilot, was eager to show off his skills to his brother. That weekend he was part of the crew of a Chinook troop-transport helicopter which

Left: As heir to the throne, Prince William will never be permitted to serve on the front line. Not so Prince Harry, who was deployed to Helmand Province, Afghanistan, as a forward air controller from December 2007. The tour was kept secret, so as not to alert the enemy to the presence of such a high-profile target.

first landed at Woolwich Barracks in South-East London to pick up Harry, before heading south to the Isle of Wight for a stag party for their cousin, Peter Phillips, prior to his marriage to Autumn Kelly on 17 May. The two princes lived up to their nickname, 'the Booze Brothers', donning matching rugby shirts reading, 'Pedro's Cowes Tour 2008' for a night on the tiles.

It later emerged that the Prince had also used a military helicopter to practise taking off and landing in a field near the Middletons' home, 'buzzed' his grandmother's and father's homes in Norfolk and Gloucestershire, and flown north to join Kate at the wedding of their friend from St Andrews, Lady Iona Douglas-Home.

While the Ministry of Defence insisted that all the training flights were authorized, an official conceded that, at a time of 'heavy operational commitments in Iraq and Afghanistan', the estimated £162,000 ($260,000) cost did not look good. The Liberal Democrat defence spokesman Nick Harvey complained that 'the public will not appreciate a military helicopter being used as a stag-do taxi service.' William, who shortly afterwards made a lightning visit to Afghanistan to meet British troops, was unapologetic, telling pensioner Mildred Francis, 'I'm working on my licence. I'm trying to do as much flying as I can. But I've been accused of wasting money – joyriding.'

Given his future choice of career – that September he announced his plan to become a search-and-rescue helicopter pilot – he must have found the criticism unwarranted. 'Joining search-and-rescue is a perfect opportunity for me to serve in the forces operationally,' he said. Unlike his brother, who had served on the front line in Afghanistan, William accepted that he would never be allowed to be a royal 'bullet-catcher'.

While he was on duty, Kate now began to stand in for him at social occasions, attending Peter Phillips's wedding at St George's Chapel, Windsor, in May – an opportunity for the Queen to take the measure of a potential future queen – followed by the marriage of Lady Rose Windsor, daughter of the Duke of Gloucester, at St James's Palace in July. At the time William was on secondment to the Royal Navy, first serving aboard the frigate HMS *Iron Duke* in the Caribbean, on patrol to catch drug smugglers, and then on attachment to a hunter-killer submarine, HMS *Talent*.

Indeed, no significant royal engagement that summer was complete without the Prince's pretty, smiling girlfriend. So, inevitably, all eyes were on her when she blurted out 'Oh my God!' on seeing her boyfriend in an ostrich-plumed hat, full-length blue velvet mantle and full regalia when he was installed as the 1,000th Knight to be appointed to the Most Noble Order of the Garter at a ceremony at Windsor Castle in June. A few days later he let his hair down as he and Kate celebrated his twenty-sixth birthday on the dance floor at the annual Beaufort Polo Club party.

Kate also appeared, with and without her man, at a charity boxing match, a louche cabaret involving a red rose and a stripper, at polo matches, tennis at Wimbledon, and at Nelson Mandela's ninetieth-birthday concert in London's Hyde Park. In September, following another holiday on Mustique with her family, she donned acid-yellow hot pants and a spangled

turquoise halterneck for a charity roller disco. When she slipped and fell flat on her backside the pictures made front-page news – much to her annoyance.

William was on two wheels a few weeks later, also for charity, but there were no photographers around to capture the spills. He and Harry took part in Enduro Africa '08, an eight-day cross-country motorcycle rally in South Africa, raising £300,000 ($488,000) for children's charities, including Harry's Project Sentebale in Lesotho. Then the Prince went below the radar for a time, joining the Special Boat Service – the Royal Navy's special-forces unit – on an undercover exercise. He returned sporting a beard – to the considerable amusement of Kate and Harry.

Not so amusing was the ever-increasing sniping, the gibes about 'Waity Katie' morphing into 'the Queen of Mustique', because she seemed to spend her days grooming, sunbathing and having fun. By the autumn of 2008 she had left her job as assistant buyer at Jigsaw and was living at home, working for her parents' company. Ironically, there was a distinct change in her social life: Boujis and other nightspots were out, Buckingham Palace and all things royal in. Kate and Harry's girlfriend, Chelsy Davy, were invited to Prince Charles's sixtieth-birthday celebrations at the Palace in November 2008, where they danced to veteran rocker Rod Stewart and mingled with celebrities like Stephen Fry, Rowan Atkinson and Joanna Lumley. While she spent Christmas with her family in Mustique, for the New Year she was the guest of Prince Charles at Birkhall in Scotland.

It was a brief romantic interlude before Prince William was back on duty again, in January 2009 transferring to RAF Shawbury in Shropshire as part of his training to become a certified Sea King pilot. Although he had managed to take a week off to join Kate and her family on the slopes at Courchevel in France in March, his seven-year romance remained firmly long distance, all the more so when Prince Harry, who was transferred to Shawbury for

helicopter training in May, joined him in the cottage he had rented
near the base. In an interview the following month, the brothers
grinned and bared all about life together, William revealing that
they did their own housework, washing-up and ironing, although
he complained that his younger brother snored. 'Oh God, they'll
think we share a bed now,' moaned Harry. 'We're brothers, not
lovers.'

Meanwhile, William's real-life lover stayed calm and carried
on, although the waiting game took a heavy toll not just on her
but on her family. Her sister Pippa was unjustly accused of using
her royal connections to help with a party-planning company
she worked for, while her brother, James, was embarrassed when
pictures of him drunk and urinating against a fence, and then
wearing his sister's polka-dot dress as well as a French maid's
outfit, were published in foreign magazines.

In August, Kate's mother was mortified still further when
her brother, Gary Goldsmith, was splashed all over *The News of
the World*, boasting of his royal connections. Undercover reporters
filmed him cutting up what appeared to be cocaine, handing out
pills that he said were Ecstasy, and offering to procure high-class
Brazilian prostitutes. Moreover, he claimed that when Kate and
William had stayed at his villa in Ibiza, suitably nicknamed 'La

Maison de Bang Bang' or The House of Sex, during the summer of 2006, he had sworn at the heir to the throne, while his friends had taught William how to mix records on DJ turntables, telling him that his catchphrase should be 'The King is in da house.'

While Gary was in da doghouse, the Prince, far from being annoyed, was nothing but sympathetic towards Kate's family. This was precisely what he had meant by the 'baggage' he attracted when he dated a young woman. Nor was Kate's long rite of passage over. In December 2009, just days after the Queen had issued a warning to the British media about intrusion into the royal family's annual holiday on the Sandringham Estate, Kate, who was staying with her family at Restormel Manor in Cornwall, found herself photographed while playing tennis on Christmas Day. The agency that sold the pictures overseas was successfully sued, her lawyers once again arguing that she was 'just a girl in the street'. By now, though, as Prince William later admitted, the couple had seriously discussed marriage.

Left: August 2009, and the reconciled William and Kate attend yet another wedding, this time that of Nicholas van Cutsem to Alice Hadden-Paton at the Guards Chapel. Despite rumours, a story-hungry media had no indication that William intended to marry Kate.

She had had to deal with this latest intrusion on her own,
for in January 2010 William flew to Australia and New Zealand
for his first official solo tour. While he good-naturedly replied
'Wait and see' to endless enquiries about his marital intentions,
patience among the media crowd was wearing thin.

Kate, who was described as living in a 'twilight' state of
limbo, like some latter-day Miss Havisham, was now accused
of 'invading her own privacy' when she appeared on the Party
Pieces website reminiscing about her own childhood cookery
experiences. The *Daily Mail* columnist Amanda Platell caught
the media's mood of disenchantment: 'Where's the proper job?
Where's the devotion to hard work and charity that are so
embedded in the life of today's favourite royals? Instead, all we
see from Kate is a stubborn protection of her privacy . . . The last
thing Britain needs is a lazy, talentless Queen of Cupcakes.'

Prince Charles alluded to the difficulties the long-suffering
Kate had undergone when he presented his son with his
provisional RAF wings at a ceremony at RAF Shawbury that

January. As Kate looked on, the Prince of Wales said: 'I know only too well how complicated it can be having a relative or close friend in the forces, because they are rarely, if ever, around. But today is a day, I think, of great pride for all of the parents, not to mention the girlfriends. We all know how hard our sons have worked in between all the other activities that we don't know about.' In a wry allusion to his son's chosen specialization as a search-and-rescue pilot, Prince Charles added: 'You will be plucking people from danger, maybe sheep in distress, not to mention endless ladies with conveniently sprained ankles on awkward mountainsides across the country.'

After a second ski holiday in Courchevel with Kate and her family, William began the final stage of his RAF career, learning to fly the Sea King helicopter, training in Cornwall, before returning to RAF Valley on the Isle of Anglesey, North Wales. Now everything was for real – in June he took part in his first mountain rescue, helping airlift a young woman who had fallen and broken her leg during a charity climb on Mount Snowdon. He did, however, take time off that month as he and his brother staged the first 'Team Wales' overseas tour, together visiting Botswana, Lesotho and South Africa, where they watched Team England grind out a poor draw with Algeria in the World Cup.

Yet even more important was 'Team Big Willies and Babykins'. While she was still officially living at home with her parents, Kate was spending more and more time with William on Anglesey, in the secluded, four-bedroomed cottage in the grounds of a country estate owned by the Meyrick family, direct descendants of Henry VIII's personal bodyguard. At last they

Above: William greeting enthusiastic members of the public in Melbourne during his visit to Australia and New Zealand in January

160

could live quietly as man and wife, shopping for pizzas and frozen chips at the local supermarket, dining on fresh crab and drinking white wine at their new local pub, the White Eagle, or heading off to their nearest cinema, the Empire in Holyhead, Kate riding pillion on the back of William's high-powered Ducati motorbike.

It was a quiet life, a normal life – and neither wanted it any other way. As a close friend explained: 'She cooks him supper, they watch TV and go to bed. It works for them. What other people would find boring, they love. They love the normalcy of it. They are very into each other.'

In September, after twenty-one months' intensive training, William finally graduated as a fully qualified RAF helicopter co-pilot and was assigned to C Flight, 22 Squadron at RAF Valley, where he will be stationed until 2013. This was the moment Kate had been waiting for.

The proposal came sooner than even she anticipated. Days after qualifying, William and Kate flew to Kenya – the country where his grandmother, then Princess Elizabeth, had learned that she was to become Queen – for a holiday on the Lewa Downs estate of his 'second family', Ian and Jane Craig. William

2010. By now Kate's name was almost as well known around the world as his own.

organized a fishing trip, the couple journeying to a rustic log cabin by a lake high on Mount Kenya. Once they arrived at the utterly remote Rutundu Lodge they did go fishing. After a fruitless afternoon they returned to their cabin where William, who had carefully carried his mother's sapphire-and-diamond engagement ring in his rucksack, formally asked Kate to be his bride. 'I literally would not let [the ring] go,' he explained later. 'Everywhere I went I was keeping hold of it. I knew if it disappeared I would be in a lot of trouble.'

Not only did his mother's ring fit perfectly, but the Prince even had a bottle of champagne chilling in the cabin's primitive outdoor cooler. 'I didn't expect it,' Kate later recalled. 'I thought he might have maybe thought about it but, no, it was a total shock when it came . . . There's a true romantic in there,' she said of her future husband.

True to form, their note in the visitors' book at the lodge gave few hints about the momentous event that had taken place. 'Thank you for such a wonderful 24 hours! Sadly no fish to be found but we had great fun trying,' wrote Kate. 'I love the warm fires and candle lights – so romantic! Hope to be back again soon. Catherine Middleton.'

At last, the waiting was over.

Right: Kate Middleton and Prince William at a friend's wedding in the summer of 2010 – only months before their own engagement finally ended all the speculation.

KATE'S STYLE

Sporting a trademark fascinator at the wedding of Laura Parker Bowles and Henry Lopes in 2006 (above), and at the wedding of Lady Rose Windsor and George Gilman in 2008 (below).

Above: Attending the Most Noble Order of the Garter procession at Windsor Castle in June 2008.

Below: At the wedding of Nicholas van Cutsem and Alice Hadden-Paton at the Guards Chapel, Wellington Barracks, in 2009.

Above: Wearing a chic beret, Kate watches the races at the Cheltenham Festival in March 2007.

Below: And opting for slightly quirkier headwear for the final day of racing at the same event in 2008.

Above: Sporting a leather cowboy hat at the Festival of British Eventing at Gatcombe Park in August 2005.

Below: Out and about in London in 2006, Kate braves the December chill in a brown casual hat.

Evening elegance: (above left) Diana at a Royal Gala Evening for the London City Ballet in 1990 and Kate at the Boodles Boxing Ball in June 2008; (above right) Diana attending the Victor Chang Charity Ball in Sydney in 1996 and Kate at the Boodles Boxing Ball for the charity Sparks in 2006.

Opposite page: (above) Diana and Kate both show a preference for British designers. Diana wearing Caroline Charles at the Braemar Games in Scotland, 1981, and Kate in a beige coat by Katherine Hooker and a Vivien Sheriff feather beret for an official engagement in February 2011.

Right: Ladies in red: Diana looks suitably regal at the Queen Mother Sports Centre in London in 1988; Kate opted for a similar style on an official visit to mark the 600th-anniversary celebrations of the University of St Andrews in February 2011.

TATLER

FEBRUARY
£3.99

Special collectors' issue

Above left: Kate's relaxed style of trademark jeans and a floral shirt in London in 2007.

Above centre: Wearing white jeans on the way to her London home in July 2007.

Above right: Sporting Hudson brand jeans to watch the princes in a charity polo match at Beaufort Polo Club in June 2008.

Bottom left: In a pretty polka-dot dress in June 2006 at the Chakravarty Polo Match at Ham Polo Club in Richmond.

Bottom centre: Walking in London in a sell-out wool dress by high-street brand French Connection.

Bottom right: Shopping in West London in a green floral dress in June 2006.

Above: Style icon in the making: Kate appears on the front cover of a special collector's edition of *Tatler* in February 2011. She is now a regular in magazine 'best dressed' lists, and is admired for her elegant yet simple style by women internationally.

WILLIAM AND CATHERINE

The Road to the Abbey

Previous pages: (left) Prince William with his fiancée, Catherine Middleton, during their visit to Belfast, Northern Ireland, in March 2011. (right) Kate during the couple's visit to their alma mater, St Andrews, to mark the 600th anniversary of the university's founding. As a wedding present, St Andrews has established a scholarship in their names.

Left: On a blustery day in February 2011, William and Kate visited Anglesey to launch an inshore lifeboat, the *Hereford Endeavour*. The visit – and especially Kate's part in it – met with widespread approval from press and public alike.

*E*ver the crowd-pleaser, she almost stole the show. Almost. For while the day belonged to Britain's future queen, Kate – or as she now wants to be called, Catherine – Middleton, William's mother was the benign spirit hovering over the couple's long-awaited engagement announcement.

To adapt Diana's famous phrase from her *Panorama* interview: there were three of them at this engagement announcement, so it was a bit crowded. Yet comforting, too. On that day, 16 November 2010, Catherine walked into the Entrée Room at St James's Palace and into a blizzard of camera flashes. Comparisons between the woman who had portentously said that she would never ascend the throne, and the girl who will one day be crowned Queen, were inevitable.

Indeed, much of Catherine's introduction to the royal goldfish bowl was reminiscent of Diana's big day in 1981, nearly thirty years earlier. The dress, the setting, the voices, even the body language, were eerily similar, while Diana's sapphire-and-diamond engagement ring took pride of place – it was, said Kate, 'very, very special'. To emphasize the inevitable comparisons, fashion photographer Mario Testino, who took the last, enchanting, black-and-white studies of Diana, shot the informal engagement photographs of the couple at St James's Palace a couple of days later.

Like Diana, Kate chose a blue dress for her engagement interview, and spoke in the well-modulated, slightly hesitant tones of a girl educated at an English private boarding school. Visibly nervous during this, her first ever TV interview, she constantly deferred to her future husband – as indeed had Diana. William was more than happy to take the lead. The one difficult moment for his bride-to-be came when she was asked the inevitable question about William's mother, Kate replying that she would have loved to have met her, before fumbling for the right words

173

ENGAGEMENTS – AND OFFICIAL ENGAGEMENTS

Far left: Princess Elizabeth during a tour of Kenya, 1 February 1952, just before her father died and she learned that she was to be Queen.

Left: Princess Elizabeth with her fiancé, the then Lieutenant Philip Mountbatten, in Edinburgh, July 1947. Like her, Kate learned she will one day be Queen in Kenya.

Bottom left: William's parents with Princess Grace of Monaco in March 1981, shortly after the announcement of their engagement.

Right: William and Catherine on their first official public appearance together following the formal announcement of their engagement, Norfolk, December 2010.

Bottom: William asked Kate to marry him in Kenya, while they were staying in a remote lodge near Lake Rutundu. They left these appreciative comments in the visitors' book.

20th - 21st October 2010.
Such fun to be back! Brought more warm clothes this time! Looked after so well, thank you guys! Look forward to next time, Soon I hope. William

Thank you for such a wonderful 24 hours! Sadly no fish to be found but we had great fun trying! I love the warm fires and candle lights - so romantic! Hope to be back again soon.
Catherine Middleton.

to complete the thought. 'She's obviously an inspirational woman to look up to,' she said.

It was almost as if she knew she was walking into a verbal minefield where every sentence concerning the late Princess might blow up in her face. Halfway through her answer she dried up, leaving William to interject. 'No one is trying to fill my mother's shoes. What she did was fantastic,' he said emphatically.

For the foreseeable future, as much as she may wish to avoid the comparison, the ghost of Diana, Princess of Wales will haunt Catherine Middleton. The very fact that William gave her his mother's engagement ring was a signal that Diana will always be part of their marriage. In his mind it was a romantic and considered gesture: 'I thought it was quite nice because obviously [Diana's] not going to be around to share any of the fun and excitement of it all. This was my way of keeping her close to it all.' Many women thought otherwise, seeing the ring as a dark omen, given Diana's tempestuous marriage and untimely death. Penny Thornton, astrologer to the late Princess, said, 'The ring will be a powerful and constant reminder of her life and death.' Nevertheless, lookalike engagement rings – not to mention reproductions of the Issa blue silk wrap dress Kate wore for her big day – sold out in hours.

For Kate, the issue was not escaping the shadow of William's mother, but living up to the expectations now resting upon her slim shoulders. Asked about becoming a royal, she said, 'It's quite a daunting prospect but hopefully I'll take it in my stride. And William's a great teacher so hopefully he'll be able to help me.' The sad irony is that Diana, who had always wanted a daughter, would, according to her former private secretary Patrick Jephson, have loved to have mentored Kate during her first few months and years in 'The Firm'.

While Kate may not have appreciated the endless comparisons with William's mother, Diana did bequeath her daughter-in-law the one thing that all the wealth and privilege in the world cannot buy – time. Unlike his father, Prince William

Above: Diana, Princess of Wales wearing the engagement ring that William gave to Kate.

had enjoyed a long – almost too long – courtship of his future wife. Their eight-year relationship contrasted with the few weeks of Charles and Diana's courtship – though they had known each other for longer. In those days, Charles was under acute pressure to marry a white, Anglo-Saxon, Protestant, aristocratic virgin.

In the intervening thirty years, the royal family has come to terms with many changes, including the Internet, mobile phones, Facebook and the right of princes – and princesses – to marry whom they choose. Prince William has grasped this opportunity, spending a year between thinking about asking Kate to marry him and actually doing so. For a time they lived virtually as man and wife in the cottage he rented near his RAF station. As he said: 'I wanted to give her a chance to see in and back out if she needed to before it all got too much. I'm trying to learn from the past. I just wanted to give her the best chance to settle in and to see what happens on the other side.'

In consequence, when William and Kate greeted the world together, they seemed more like a couple who had been married for years. They appeared comfortable with each other, knowing all each other's jokes and stories and which side of the bed each sleeps on. 'When I first met Kate I knew there was something very special about her,' he recalled. 'I knew there was

Right: The cottage on Anglesey, where Prince William is stationed as a serving pilot, where he and Catherine will begin their married life.

possibly something that I wanted to explore there. We ended up being friends for a while and that was a good foundation.' Their relationship had all the right ingredients for longevity: a couple happy and in love, and with none of the metaphysical equivocation that Prince Charles had showed when, in his engagement interview, he was asked about his feelings. 'Whatever "in love" means,' was his now infamous reply. His son was clear and forthright: 'We are hugely excited and looking forward to spending the rest of our lives together.'

William's mature, assured performance also stood in contrast to his father's rather churlish reaction when asked about the impending nuptials. 'He's been practising for a long time!' he said

Below: William and Catherine on their way to the photo call in the State Rooms at St James's Palace on the day their engagement was formally announced.

of his son. While the Queen and Kate's parents had expressed their delight, and Harry had mused, 'It means I get a sister, which I have always wanted,' the Prince of Wales seemed a forlorn side figure, ungracious and curmudgeonly. Perhaps unsurprisingly, opinion polls the weekend after the announcement all suggested, as they have for some years, that on the Queen's death the Crown should skip a generation and pass straight to William. Much as William may have bridled, the fact was that at the time between one half and two thirds of the public wanted the newlyweds to be the next King and Queen.

Just as the engagement day illustrated the character differences between father and son, so the way William planned the announcement gave an insight into his royal style. Instinctively suspicious of the outside world, he has learned to keep his own counsel. This was just as well, for the engagement announcement was delayed due to the death of Kate's beloved grandfather, Peter Middleton, in early November, aged ninety.

The engagement was such a closely guarded secret that, although William had formally asked for Michael Middleton's consent, Kate was unsure whether her mother knew – and hesitated before breaking the news. (Carole, naturally was 'over the moon'.) Significantly, both the Queen and Prince Charles were told only a few hours beforehand. 'He wants to be in control of everything to do with his life,' noted a former royal official.

Once the excitement was over it was back to business as usual, William reporting for duty at his RAF station in Anglesey. Within days he and his four-man crew were in action, rescuing a climber who had a suspected heart attack on Mount Snowdon. Meanwhile Kate stayed at her parents' house in Berkshire, planning the wedding. For her, though, life would never be the same again, as demonstrated by the wary-eyed woman sitting next to her when she drove away from her parents' house. The female bodyguard was one of a three-strong armed protection squad detailed to guard the future Queen around the clock. As a former royal 'bullet catcher' noted: 'Their presence is a constant reminder that Kate is different. She is now a potential target.'

To help Kate cope with the transition, William had asked courtiers to give her advice if he was working. Clearly the couple, as William had said during their interview, had learned lessons from the past. He asked Sir David Manning, formerly Britain's

Ambassador to the United States, to give Kate lessons in protocol and the intricacies of royal life. Also on hand was Camilla, who took Kate out to lunch during the engagement, giving her another perspective on life in the goldfish bowl.

It had been so different when Diana became engaged. She had moved away from her family and friends to live with the Queen Mother at Clarence House until the wedding day. As a result, she had felt isolated and alone, unsure how to act and whom to ask for help. If anything, her first official public appearance had been even more of an ordeal than the engagement day. She chose a black ballgown with plunging, gravity defying décolletage, which had commentators wondering if she had exposed more than she should, for a charity gala in the presence of Princess Grace of Monaco, the former Hollywood star Grace Kelly. 'It was an horrendous occasion,' she later told me. 'I didn't know whether to go out of the door first. I didn't know whether your handbag should be in your left hand not your right hand. I was terrified, really – at the time everything was all over the place.' Sensing her discomfort, Princess Grace took her aside and listened as she poured out her heart. 'Don't worry,' Princess Grace had joked, 'it will get a lot worse.'

There was no such exposure, either physical or public, when Kate undertook her first official engagement, a low-key, understated affair in keeping with the couple's approach to the wedding and, it might be said, with their own royal lifestyle. In December they watched the Thursford Christmas Spectacular in Norfolk, and afterwards attended a special reception in aid of the Teenage Cancer Trust at the invitation of Emilie van Cutsem, chairman of the charity appeal and a close friend of the royal family. The crowds were modest, as was the future Queen's attire; on a chilly evening there was not a hint of décolletage, Kate wearing a sensible knee-length black-and-white dress.

Above: Having her own security detail 24/7 is now a fact of Kate Middleton's life. She is seen here at a friend's wedding in January 2011 with Karen Llewellyn, a member of her police protection detail.

It was sixty-eight days before the couple appeared together
in public again – after all, they had a wedding to plan. First, there
was the date, which they wanted to be as soon as possible so
that they could resume 'normal' life. After consulting with the
Queen, the Prime Minister and other significant figures they
plumped for Friday, 29 April, which is, by happy coincidence,
also the feast day of St Catherine of Siena. More than just a
royal wedding, for many people the event offered the chance to
enjoy a four-day break, given the existing public holiday on 1
May and the government's decision to make the wedding day
officially another.

There were soon plenty of unofficial souvenirs and other
memorabilia for those wanting to get into the wedding-day spirit.
After donning their official T-shirts, and perhaps applying 'No
More Waity Katie' lip gloss and nail varnish, they could sit down
and watch saturation global TV coverage – more than a billion
people were expected to tune in – while drinking a cheering
cuppa made from William and Kate tea bags. For something
stronger, they might choose the specially concocted 'Fashionably
Kate' cocktail or Kiss Me Kate ale, while for the wedding night

itself there were even Crown Jewels condoms. As for those for whom the whole business was all too much, the artist Lydia Leith designed royal-wedding sick-bags under the title 'Throne Up'.

Meanwhile, away from bone-china royal-wedding thimbles, iPad cases and commemorative coins, there was the serious matter of choosing the church. While Charles and Diana had picked St Paul's Cathedral, most other royal weddings, coronations and funerals, notably that of the late Diana, Princess of Wales, have taken place at Westminster Abbey. It is the final resting place of seventeen kings and queens, while the present Queen, Princess Margaret, the Princess Royal and the Duke of York were all married there. Royal aides said that the couple had chosen Westminster Abbey because of its 'staggering beauty, its thousand years of royal history and its relative intimacy despite its size.'

It was appropriate, too, that the service was scheduled to be conducted by three senior churchmen: the Dean of Westminster, Dr John Hall, who would conduct the service; the Archbishop of Canterbury, Dr Rowan Williams, who would perform the marriage ceremony, in keeping with royal tradition; while the Bishop of London, the Right Rev Richard Chartres, a friend of the royal family who gave the address at the thanksgiving service for Diana, Princess of Wales, was asked to give the address.

With the formalities completed, it would be time to celebrate. It was fortunate that the groom's grandmother has a decent-sized palace just down the Mall where their guests could toast the newlyweds because, for once, a marquee in the Middletons' garden would not suffice. Unlike previous royal weddings, though, William and Kate wanted a more informal celebration. Instead of a wedding breakfast, they decided on a luncheon reception, hosted by the Queen, at Buckingham Palace for 600 guests, all drawn from the congregation, and representing the couple's personal and public lives. That evening, Prince Charles would host a dinner for 300 family and friends, followed by dancing. As with every wedding, the trickiest decisions concerned the guest list – whom to leave in and whom to leave out. Numbers at the abbey were limited to 1,900. Unlike an ordinary wedding, however, the Foreign Office, the Lord Chamberlain's Office, which sends out the invitations, and the Vice-Marshal of the Diplomatic Corps were all intimately involved in approving the final guest list.

Right: Turning in another faultless performance: Kate during her visit to Northern Ireland with William in March 2011.

ROYAL WEDDINGS
1840–1986

Right: Queen Victoria marries Prince Albert of Saxe-Coburg and Gotha at the Chapel Royal, St James's Palace, in February 1840. A contemporary observer wrote: 'Her dress was a rich white satin, trimmed with orange blossoms, and upon her head she wore a wreath of the same beautiful flowers.'

Below: The marriage of Princess Elizabeth (now Queen Elizabeth II) to Philip Mountbatten took place at Westminster Abbey on 20 November 1947, a time of shortages in Britain following the end of the Second World War.

Above right: The marriage of Lady Elizabeth Bowes-Lyon to Prince Albert, Duke of York, 26 April 1923 – the couple, aware of the austerity of the times, aimed for as low-key an affair as possible. At right are King George V and his wife, Queen Mary; the newlyweds were, of course, to become better known as King George VI and Queen Elizabeth the Queen Mother.

Far right: Prince William's parents, Prince Charles and Lady Diana Spencer, were married at St Paul's Cathedral on 29 July 1981, an event that attracted enormous attention throughout the world.

Following page: (top left) The Queen's sister, Princess Margaret, travels to her wedding in the Glass Coach, accompanied by the Duke of Edinburgh, 6 May 1960.

———— •:• ————

(top right): William's mother on her way to St Paul's and marriage to the Prince of Wales, 29 July 1981. The train of her dress was so long that, in the carriage, it had to be piled on her father, Earl Spencer's lap.

———— •:• ————

(bottom) As Diana arrived at St Paul's Cathedral for the ceremony a gust of wind caused some problems for the bridesmaids trying to keep the train under control.

Right: Two photographs of William, then aged four, as a page boy during the wedding service for his uncle, Prince Andrew, and Sarah Ferguson at Westminster Abbey, 23 July 1986. Andrew was appointed Duke of York on the day of his marriage.

Below: The new Duke and Duchess of York leave Buckingham Palace for their honeymoon in a carriage and a cloud of confetti.

Besides a thousand or so friends and family – Kate's colourful uncle Gary Goldsmith was in, while the disgraced Sarah, Duchess of York, who was caught out offering cash for access to her ex-husband, Prince Andrew, was out – the couple had to find room for members of foreign royal families, Governors-General, Commonwealth prime ministers, as well as members of the government, the military, the Diplomatic Corps, and representatives from charities. As the wedding was deemed to be a semi-state, somewhat informal, occasion, there was no invitation for President Sarkozy of France and his glamorous wife, Carla Bruni, or for Barack and Michelle Obama. One high-octane couple who did get the nod were football star David Beckham and his designer wife, Victoria. William, as President of the Football Association, had become friendly with the one-time king of football in Switzerland in December 2010, during England's disastrous bid to stage the 2018 World Cup.

As well as to the gilded and high-born, invitations went out to the butcher, the postman and the pub landlord from Kate's village in Berkshire, a clear sign that she – and her mother – were keeping a close eye on the arrangements. After all, together with the Queen and Prince Charles, the Middletons had agreed to share the cost of the wedding, excluding policing, which was paid from the public purse. This led to some brisk questioning in the media about how the they were able to afford it. It emerged that

Below: David Beckham with William in Zurich for the announcement of the 2018 Football World Cup, December 2010. Despite the support and presence of the Prince and the world-famous footballer – as well as the Prime Minister, David Cameron – England's bid ended in abject failure.

Above: Pippa Middleton at a VIP event at Somerset House, London, in November 2009.

not only did their company, Party Pieces, sell balloons, party hats and other items for successful children's events, but it made a small fortune from selling its database of well-off young mothers to mail-order and other companies for up to £20,000 ($32,500) a time.

This was just as well because, besides hiring Westminster Abbey, the Middleton clan were taking over an entire Belgravia hotel, The Goring, which is situated just the other side of the walls of Buckingham Palace. Here Kate would spend her last night as a single woman, in the company of her family, including her sister Pippa, chosen as her Maid of Honour, and where the four bridesmaids and two pageboys – all from William's side of the family – would gather.

While the couple, in the modern fashion, established their own wedding website, Kate insisted on keeping the style and the designer of her wedding dress a closely guarded secret. That did not stop intense speculation. Front-runners included Bruce Oldfield, a favourite of Diana, Princess of Wales, especially after Carole and Pippa Middleton were seen at his Knightsbridge store, and Sarah Burton, creative director at Alexander McQueen, who had designed the strapless silk gown for the 2005 wedding of Sarah Buys and Camilla's son, Tom Parker Bowles.

Fashion mavens thought that the choice of Burton would give Kate an edgier, more fashion-forward look than hitherto. Not edgy enough, however, for the veteran British designer Vivienne Westwood, who declared during London Fashion Week in February 2011, 'I would have loved to dress Kate Middleton but I have to wait until she kind of catches up a bit somewhere with style.'

That was not quite how women on both sides of the Atlantic saw Kate's emerging fashion sense. During the run-up to the

wedding, every piece she had chosen to wear proved a sell-out on the British High Street – and on Madison Avenue. In New York, Kate's glossy, groomed yet stylishly affordable look resonated with young American women. Brand director Andy Rogers of Reiss, who supplied several of her understated dresses, felt that, like First Lady Michelle Obama, Kate has the knack of expressing herself by mixing designer labels with high-street brands. 'She is stylish in affordable clothes and accessories,' he said. Quietly and confidently, she was forging her own distinctive style, the comparisons with Diana becoming less and less frequent as the months went by. When the see-through dress which Kate had modelled during the now famous college fashion show was sold at auction in March for £78,000 ($125,000) her emerging iconic status was confirmed.

Unlike Diana, who had been apprehensive and nervous during her first forays into public life, Kate seemed to be having fun. Certainly, albeit after an understandably nervy start with her first TV interview, the future royal got into her stride, although, admittedly, her first engagements were deliberately kept relaxed and low-key.

In late February she dipped her toe in the water when she and William launched an inshore lifeboat before a crowd of about a thousand in Anglesey, where the couple will initially make their home. Little touches, such as the fact that she had had her Katherine Hooker herringbone coat shortened, in tune with an age of austerity, and that the fascinator she wore instead of a hat was adorned with the insignia of the Royal Welch Fusiliers, appropriate for a visit to Wales, won approval from the watching fashion police.

That same month, her second royal engagement took her back to St Andrews, where she and William chatted with students, professors and even their former cleaner. 'This is a very special moment for Catherine and me. It feels like coming home,' William told the audience as he officially launched the university's six-hundredth-anniversary charity appeal. Later, the couple signed a book of condolence for the victims of the earthquake in New Zealand at the country's High Commission in London. Then, early in March, he and Kate flew unannounced to Belfast in Northern Ireland, thereby completing their tour of the four countries making up the Union. In celebration of Shrove

Tuesday, they successfully flipped pancakes before a small crowd of well-wishers, Kate proving rather more adept than her fiancé.

William showed another safe pair of hands during a trip to New Zealand and Australia in March, in the course of which he visited Christchurch, the city most affected by the tragedy, before travelling on to Australia to visit Queensland and Victoria, which had been devastated by recent flooding. A royal spokesman said: 'The Royal Family have been watching the natural disasters with the same shock and sadness as everyone else. They wanted to show their solidarity with the people of New Zealand and Australia.' His humility, his willingness to listen as survivors told their stories, and his approachability had the local media calling him 'the Prince of Hearts' and, inevitably, 'the People's Prince'. As one headline put it, 'Long it rained and long may he.'

Diana would have been very proud.

Right: The future Princess of Wales, looking every inch the queen she will one day become. St Andrews, Scotland, 25 February 2011.

WILLIAM AND CATHERINE

The Wedding Day

*I*t was a day to cherish. A day to look back on with fondness and with pride. Amid the heart-stopping spectacle and the pomp and circumstance, it was very much a family occasion. While the 1,900-strong congregation of royals, diplomats, friends and celebrities absorbed the spine-tingling moment when Catherine Middleton appeared at the West Door of Westminster Abbey, her mother Carole just about managed to stem the tear poised to roll down her right cheek. 'You're so beautiful,' whispered William the moment he first saw his bride after her long slow walk down the aisle on the arm of her father Michael. Crowned with a kiss on the balcony at Buckingham Palace – 'Oh wow,' said the new bride when she saw the sea of people on the Mall cheering and waving flags – it was the newly minted Duchess of Cambridge who was the undoubted star of the show. She had woken up a commoner in a bedroom at the Goring Hotel, and went to sleep – after an evening of revelry – a duchess, in a suite at Buckingham Palace.

On a day of bright-eyed tears, laughter and happy faces, the memory of the late Diana, Princess of Wales was in the minds and hearts of many. As one woman spectator remarked, 'When the sun came out just as Kate reached the altar we knew it was Diana.' True or not, the wedding marked a new chapter not only in the lives of William and Catherine but of the royal family, the hour-long marriage ceremony not just the union of two young people, but a renewal of the historic compact between the nation and the monarchy. The memories of the September day in 1997 when William and Harry walked solemnly behind their mother's funeral cortège were now overlaid by the sight of the smiling young Prince, hand in hand with his enchanting bride, returning along that same route in the 1902 State Landau to Buckingham Palace, ready to begin a new life together.

The relaxed, almost low-key approach to the big day –

Left: Prince William in the striking scarlet of the Colonel of the Irish Guards, and his brother Harry, a captain in the Blues and Royals, enter the abbey.

watched by an estimated television audience of 2.4 billion – was exemplified the night before when William decided at the last minute to go on a short walkabout, meeting and greeting well-wishers camped outside Clarence House. Catherine was awake early. She hid her nerves beneath jokey banter, instructing her hairdresser Richard Ward that his only job was to ensure that her auburn locks were styled in such a way that 'by the time she got to the altar William must be able to recognize her'. Meanwhile her brother James had travelled the short distance to Clarence House for breakfast with his future brothers-in-law before they dressed in their military uniforms, Harry as a captain of the Blues and Royals, his regiment, and William in the striking scarlet uniform of the Colonel of the Irish Guards, a position to which he had been appointed in February.

She had other wedding gifts to bestow, showering the Prince and his bride-to-be with a confetti of titles. Before William left Clarence House with his best man, he had become His Royal Highness the Duke of Cambridge, Earl of Strathearn and Baron Carrickfergus. Plain Catherine was on her way to becoming Her Royal Highness the Duchess of Cambridge. Meanwhile her mother, who was the first member of the Middleton family to leave for Westminster Abbey, showed where her daughter gained her poised fashion sense, looking sophisticated and stylish in a sky-blue crêpe coatdress and day dress by Diana's favourite designer, Catherine Walker. With a nod to her local roots her matching hat was by Berkshire-based Jane Corbett.

But it was her youngest daughter, Pippa, who really caught the eye, the fashion police and the international Twitterati

Below: A jolly moment that typifies a beautiful day, as bridesmaids and pageboys find something to make them giggle.

going wild with admiration for the Maid of Honour's ivory vintage-style dress. Pippa, who kept the four bridesmaids and two pageboys well marshalled, was but the hors d'oeuvre for the fashion banquet to come. There was an audible gasp from the congregation, which included David and Victoria Beckham, a fashion designer herself, singer Sir Elton John, comedian Rowan Atkinson, Australian Olympic swimmer Ian Thorpe, film director Guy Ritchie, as well as European royalty, diplomats and politicians, when Catherine arrived at the abbey in a royal Rolls-Royce Phantom VI. The best-kept secret of the wedding was finally unveiled: the dress. As with other royal wedding dresses, it is instantly iconic and historic, marking not just the character of the wearer but the tenor of the times.

Nor did Catherine let anyone down. The girl who has been criticized for being too conservatively High Street chose the doyenne of the fashion world, Sarah Burton of the British house Alexander McQueen, to speak for her, her dress elegant,

Below: The Queen and Prince Philip are preceded by Prince Charles and Camilla as they are led to their places on arrival at the abbey.

Right: Pippa Middleton, Maid of Honour, looked stunning in her vintage-style dress designed by Sarah Burton.

understated, beautifully balancing tradition with modernity, quintessentially feminine. The bride had worked closely with Burton, who has a reputation for meticulous craftsmanship, and who also designed her sister's dress. The designer later said: 'It's been the experience of a lifetime to work with Catherine Middleton to create her wedding dress and I have enjoyed every moment of it.'

The dress, which echoed the gown worn by the Duchess of York – later Queen Elizabeth the Queen Mother, on her wedding day in 1923, was complemented by the Cartier halo tiara which the Queen had loaned for the occasion. The tiara, made in 1936, was a gift of the then Duke of York – his life made famous by the Oscar-winning movie *The King's Speech* – to his bride three weeks before he succeeded his brother as King. If Catherine was sending out a message, it was that she would support her husband through thick and thin, just as the new Queen Elizabeth had done when her stammering husband took his first tremulous steps as King George VI.

A sign, too, that her family would be an integral part of her new life was perhaps demonstrated by the fact that she wore diamond-set stylized oak-leaf earrings, based on the Middleton family's new coat of arms, which her parents gave for her wedding day. Symbolism aside, Catherine looked simply sensational, all eyes on the radiant beauty as she walked down the aisle through the arbor of maple trees to the moving 'I Was Glad' by Sir Hubert Parry, which had first been sung at the coronation of Edward Vll in 1902. The couple had spent hours choosing the music, which was mainly by well-known British composers like Ralph Vaughan Williams, with the help of Prince Charles.

As Catherine slowly made her way to the altar, first Harry then William sneaked a brief glance at the bride. William was not disappointed, clearly moved by the vision standing before him. Then the part to test the nerves: taking the vows that would seal their love.

It was difficult to gauge which betrayed the greater nervousness, William's throaty 'I will', or Catherine's rather weak, tremulous voice as she repeated her future husband's full names, William Arthur Philip Louis, in formal response to the Archbishop of Canterbury, the Most Reverend Dr Rowan Williams, who was one of three leading churchmen to officiate; the Dean of Westminster, the Very Reverend Dr John Hall, and the Right Reverend Dr Richard Chartres, Bishop of London respectively introducing the service and giving the address. The memory of Diana, who famously muddled up Charles's Christian names, will have been vividly in her mind. Catherine did not, however, promise to obey her man. The immediate ordeal over, she remained quivering as she and her husband sat together listening to the Bishop of London's address. He spoke of love, celebration and the joys of family life. It was another member of the Middleton family, Catherine's younger brother James, who also impressed, showing few nerves as he gave a strong-voiced reading of the lesson from Romans: 12.

While everyone played their full part, it was clear that, understandable nerves aside, the couple were the determined master and mistress not merely of the day, but of their destiny. The prayer they wrote for the occasion symbolized their sense of purpose: 'In the busyness of each day keep our eyes fixed on what is real and important in life and help us to be generous with our time and love and energy.' Dr Williams, who had spent time with the couple before the event, discussing the importance of the day, emphasized their uncomplicated unity of purpose: 'They've thought through what they want for themselves, but also what they want to say. They've had a simple, very direct picture of what really matters about this event. I think that they have a clear sense of what they believe they're responsible to.' Describing them as 'deeply unpretentious' people, he stressed, in a clear reference to past mistakes, that such a public commitment was not without its perils. 'They're sensible, realistic young people. They know what the cost of that might be. They've thought that through. And because of that they will need the support, the solidarity and the prayers of all those who are watching today.'

Right: Carole Middleton, mother of the bride, looking calm and elegant in sky blue as she arrives at the abbey.

Following pages: The bride, the dress, the train and the Maid of Honour, just before entering Westminster Abbey. Nothing in any of these elements disappointed the watching billions.

Judging by the rolling crescendo of cheering when they appeared at the West Door of the abbey, they had all the support they needed. The huge crowds outside, and in Hyde Park watching giant screens, had sung along lustily to enduring British hymns like 'Guide Me, O Thou Great Redeemer' – in remembrance of Diana, for it had been sung at her funeral – and 'Love Divine, All Loves Excelling', finished off by the 'other' national anthem, the rousing 'Jerusalem', with its words by William Blake and set to music by Parry.

While they were bathed in rowdy affection, no chances were taken, a wary-eyed and armed policeman in the heavy gold-braided uniform of a postillion riding shotgun immediately behind them on their coach journey in the 1902 State Landau down the Mall to Buckingham Palace. As the royal couple waited for guests to join them for a champagne reception, hosted by the Queen, they had time to pose for portraits for their private album taken by Hugo Burnand, who also shot the pictures at the wedding of Prince Charles to Camilla Parker Bowles. Then it was the moment everyone had been waiting for; the kiss.

As the couple made their way out on to the balcony, the new Duchess looked rather overwhelmed by the exuberant sea of humanity before her, for the entire Mall in front of the Palace was jammed with spectators. She was joined moments later by the Middleton clan and the rest of the royal family. Her mother instinctively made to wave to the cheering crowd, but quickly stopped herself once she saw that the Queen kept her hands to her sides. Yet although this was a once-in-a-lifetime experience for the Middletons, it was also one to which HRH the Duchess of Cambridge will soon become accustomed.

Unlike the first famous balcony kiss, when Charles had asked his mother 'May I?' before kissing Diana, William needed no bidding, kissing his bride not once but twice, much to the delight of the crowd and the eager photographers. After watching a spectacular flypast by Second World War-vintage aircraft and modern fighter jets, he and his bride chatted to some of the 600 guests. Then they left for Clarence House, William driving his father's vintage blue Aston Martin Volante, for time alone before the evening festivities. Harry was the chief suspect behind the learner-driver's 'L'-plate and the trailing metallic balloons that partially covered the 'Just Wed' number-plate. The younger prince was at his mischievous best that night when the most intimate group of the day, 300 family and friends, turned the Palace into a disco, the mood set by Harry's irreverent best-man's speech.

Late that night the Duke and Duchess floated to bed at Buckingham Palace on a sea of goodwill and good wishes. As for most newlyweds, their honeymoon was to be a time of relaxation and recuperation. Thereafter the hard work begins. They may be

Below: Catherine and her father, Michael Middleton, arrive at the altar, where William and his best man are already waiting.

at the start-line of life as a married couple but, if their wedding day is any guide, they are well equipped for the journey before them. They met as friends, became lovers, and are now the most celebrated royal couple on earth, invested with the magic of monarchy and surrounded by the goodwill of the people.

In Catherine it is clear that William, sometimes reluctant to accept his responsibility as a future king, has found a companion who has resolve, patience, loyalty and imagination. As her wedding dress suggests, she has perhaps chosen to model herself on Queen Elizabeth the Queen Mother, who is often credited with saving the monarchy from self-destruction following the Abdication crisis. Like her mother and her grandmother, 'Lady Dorothy', she has a steely determination behind the eternal smile.

Catherine once said that William was lucky to have her. Given her faultless display on the biggest day of her life, the same might be said of the monarchy.

Below: The moment for which so many had waited, and had so eagerly anticipated – William places the band of Welsh gold on his bride's finger.

Left: The new Duke and his Duchess emerge from the abbey to a thunderous reception from the watching crowd.

Right: Safely seated in the 1902 State Landau for the journey back to Buckingham Palace.

Below: The Queen and Prince Philip leave the abbey for the Palace in the Glass Coach.

High fashion meets high society. Guests included: (clockwise, from top left) Tara Palmer-Tomkinson and her sister Santa Montefiore; Princess Beatrice of York and her sister Princess Eugenie; Miriam Gonzalez Durantez, wife of the Deputy Prime Minister Nick Clegg; Crown Princess Victoria of Sweden and Prince Daniel of Sweden; Chelsy Davy; Zara Phillips and her sister-in-law Autumn Phillips; Sir Elton John; James Middleton; Prime Minister David Cameron and his wife Samantha; David and Victoria Beckham; Earl Spencer and Karen Gordon.

Well-wishers in Parliament Square before the wedding (above); (below) the street party in Clarence Street, Southall, West London – the street where Catherine's maternal grandparents once lived.

Some came from thousands of miles away (above centre and right); others held street parties in celebration at home – Harberton Road, North London.

Above: The carriage drive to the
Palace down the Mall, with an escort
from the Household Cavalry.

Below: Michael and Carole Middleton
– clearly more relaxed after the
ceremony – smiling at the cheering
crowds.

Above: Pippa travelled to the Palace in an open carriage with two of the bridesmaids and one of the pages . . .

Below: . . . while Prince Harry travelled with the others.

Left: Policemen salute as the
State Landau enters the gates of
Buckingham Palace.

Above: The newlyweds arrive at
the Grand Entrance at the back of
Buckingham Palace, which is out of
the sight of the crowds.

Above: The moment the world had been waiting for. William and Catherine kiss on the balcony of Buckingham Palace.

Right: Hawker Hurricane (left) and Supermarine Spitfire fighters flank an Avro Lancaster bomber during the flypast by the RAF's Battle of Britain flight while the couple were on the Palace balcony.

ACKNOWLEDGEMENTS AND PHOTO CREDITS

This has been a fascinating book to research and write. It was for me a chance to rekindle old friendships and make new ones. As is normal with books about royalty, some people have asked to remain anonymous, but I would like to thank the following for their insights and memories: Lisa Agar, Michael Choong, Max Ciscotti, Michael Fidler, Tony Humphrey, Patrick Jephson, Jennifer Kelly, Shirley Kneath, Dr Brian Lang, Julia Leake, Matt May, Andrew Neil, Dave Philpot, Peter Ratcliffe, Emma Sayle, Dr David Starkey, Penny Thornton, Lynda Tillotson, Ken Wharfe, Gemma Williamson, Connie Woodbridge and Thomas Woodcock. I would also like to thank my team of researchers for their endeavours under considerable time constraints: Mydrim Jones, Ali and Lydia Morton, Nic North, Tom Rayner and Irene Thompson. I am grateful, too, as always, to Hope Dellon of St Martin's Press, New York, and to Rosie Baring, Councillor Julian Bell, Annabel Buchan, Faye Caten, Patrick Knowles, Ned Stileman, Dominique Tweedsmuir and Nick York. At Michael O'Mara Books I would like to thank Louise Dixon and George Maudsley, as well as Ana McLaughlin for organizing a publicity schedule to die for, my editor Toby Buchan for his prodigious memory, work rate and sangfroid, Judith Palmer for winkling out royal pictures the world has rarely seen, and Ana Bježančević for designing an elegant tribute to the young royal couple about to set off on life's journey together. Good luck to them both.